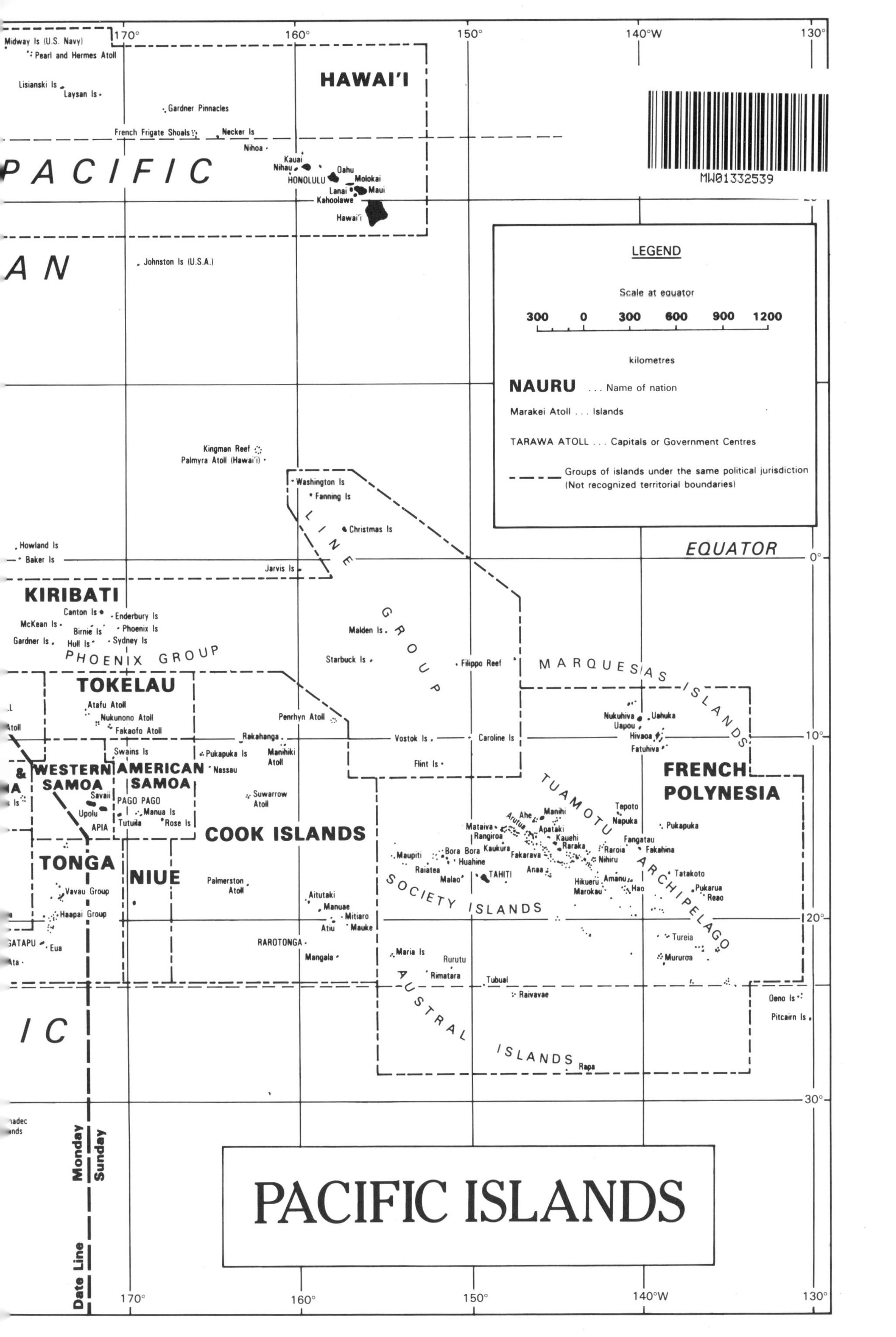

PACIFIC ISLANDS

The Pacific in the 20th Century

Pacific People and Society

Martin Peake

Cambridge University Press
Cambridge
New York Port Chester Melbourne Sydney

Published by the Press Syndicate of the University of Cambridge
The Pitt Building, Trumpington Street, Cambridge CB2 1RP, UK
40 West 20th Street, New York, NY 10011, USA
10 Stamford Road, Oakleigh, Melbourne 3166, Australia

First published 1991

Printed in Hong Kong by Colorcraft

National Library of Australia cataloguing-in-publication data:

Peake, Martin.
Pacific people and society.

Includes index.
ISBN 0 521 37628 9.

1. Oceania — Foreign relations — United States.
2. United States — Foreign relations — Oceania.
I. Title. (Series : Pacific in the twentieth century).

327.9073

Contents

Acknowledgements

The author would like to thank Karen von Strokirch for her helpful suggestions during the preparation of this book, and Nick Maclellan for his support in obtaining many of the photographs.

The author and publisher are grateful to the following for permission to reproduce copyright material. (Short extracts come from material in the 'Resources' list for each chapter.)

ABC Radio for extract from 'Background Briefing', 1983; The *Age*; Agence France Presse; Alladin Books Ltd and Greenpeace Communications Ltd for photograph of *Greenpeace* from *The Nuclear Arms Race*, 1986; Allen & Unwin Australia for map from *White Women in Fiji* by Claudia Knapman, 1986; The *Australian*; Deakin University Press for illustration from *Unwritten Knowledge* by L. Farrell, 1984; *Fiji Times*; *Fiji Sun*; Friends of the Earth for diagrams from *The Nuclear Environment* by L. Dalton; Dewe Gorodey for interview in *South Pacific Dossier*, Wood, G. (ed.); Paul Greco; Harper Collins Publishers, London for photograph from *Maralinga* by A. Tame and F. Robotham, 1986; Giff Johnson; The Herald and Weekly Times; M. Knight; N. Maclellan; Maxwell Macmillan Pergamon Publishing Australia Pty Ltd for material from *We, the Navigators* by D. Lewis; Micronesian Support Centre, Honolulu; Nuclear Free and Independent Pacific; Novosti Press Agency, Moscow; Denis O'Rourke; *Pacific Island Monthly Magazine*, Suva; *Pacific Report* for extracts from Issue No. 5, 1988; *Pacific Viewpoint* for extracts from 'Mobility and Identity in the Island Pacific', Vol. 26, No. 1, 1985, and 'Pacific Perspective, Pacific Identity', Vol. 12, 1984; Peace Research Centre, Research School of Pacific Studies, for extract from *New Caledonia: Anti-colonialism in a Pacific Territory* by Helen Fraser; Pilot Printing and Publishing Ltd, Auckland for chart from *For Kanak Independence, the Fight Against French Rule in New Caledonia* by S. Ounei, 1985; Solomon Islands Women Writers for 'Women and Housework' by Lemu Darcy and 'Working Mother' by Jully Sipolo from *Mi Mere: Poetry and Prose*, A. Billy, H. Lulei & J. Sipolo (eds); South Pacific Social Sciences Association, Fiji for 'Literate Societies' from 'Pacific Perspective, Pacific Identity'; *Sydney Morning Herald*; Taylor & Francis Ltd for map and extracts from *S.I.P.R.I. Year Book, 1980*; Konai Thaman for the poem 'U.S.A. Encounter'; Uniting Church of Australia, Division of Social Justice for extract from 'Kanaky after Tjibaou?' *Pacific Issues*, 1989; United Press International; United States Government Printing Office; University of Chicago Press and Routledge & Kegan Paul, London for diagrams from *Art of Memory* by F. Yates; Victorian Association of Peace Studies for diagram from 'A Future for the South Pacific — Nuclear Free' by M. Hamel-Green *Peace Dossier 8*.

While every care has been taken to trace and acknowledge copyright, in some cases this has not been possible. The publishers would welcome any information which would assist in redressing the situation.

INTRODUCTION

This is one of three books in the series **The Pacific in the 20th Century**. They have been specifically written for middle secondary students. Each of the three books in the series examines a different aspect of the Pacific. *Pacific People and Place* covers the geography of the islands and issues related to development. *Pacific People and Change* covers key events and changes occurring in the recent history of the islands. *Pacific People and Society* examines issues which affect individuals, groups and communities in the islands.

At a time when people on the rim are trying to learn more about the islands and peoples of the Pacific, this series of books takes an important step forward in increasing our level of understanding and in combating ignorance of one of the major regions of the world.

Pacific People and Society examines key social, political and cultural questions facing many Pacific Island nations. The Pacific is changing rapidly and the consequences are transforming the region on many levels. Each chapter in the text is designed to give students access to the causes of change and a critical understanding of why the coups in Fiji and the fighting on New Caledonia occur and the possible outcomes of these events.

The chapters use the inquiry method, and from information given in each chapter, conflicting opinions, maps, pictures and guides, students can quickly begin to recognise how important the Pacific is and how rapidly technology and other factors affect the small nations there.

The text highlights the struggles of the two superpowers trying to outmanoeuvre each other over the vast Pacific Ocean for some strategic advantage. The opening chapter investigates the following questions: Is there a Soviet threat? Is the Pacific an American lake? How will the warming of relations between the Soviet Union and the United States affect Pacific Island nations? What happens when New Zealand bans nuclear-armed and powered warships? These and other important issues are examined, bringing students to a critical and comprehensive understanding of superpower rivalry.

Another chapter examines the independence struggle in New Caledonia by the indigenous Kanaks who have staged a determined war against the French nationals. Both sides of the conflict are presented and the strategies each uses to help their cause and to influence future outcomes is examined in detail.

Another chapter looks at the tragic consequences of ten years of nuclear testing in the Marshall Islands. It shows how the United States was able to persuade the local inhabitants of Bikini Atoll to give their land over for testing for 'the good of mankind and to end all wars'. Fifty years later the deadly radiation still prevents the Bikinians from returning to the atoll. This chapter shows the legacy of a displaced people whose culture has been devastated and raises issues of basic human rights for the students to consider.

The preservation of Pacific Island culture is also introduced to students through a case study of an orally transmitted navigation system. The navigators could make long voyages without compasses and arrive with pinpoint accuracy at atolls hundreds of kilometres away. Their secret knowledge was never written, but passed down by master navigators to the next generation. How has modern technology changed the status of the navigators? Will their tradition continue or will it be absorbed into Western culture?

Students should develop, through using this book, a critical understanding of political, cultural and social issues which pertain to the emerging Pacific Island nations and, within a general social science framework, apply the skills and methodology to key questions and issues about the Pacific. The initial focus question is followed by a brief introductory passage and a list of related questions. These provide the student with a guide to the information and materials they will be working with later in the chapter. There are also activities within the main body of the text. They have sequential development, beginning with comprehensive-based activities which are followed by activities which require more logic, analysis and methodological development.

A student's inquiry into *Pacific People and Society* would benefit from several teacher-directed lessons, the screening of films, and visits by speakers planned for the purpose of offering alternative case studies.

Martin Peake

SUPERPOWER RIVALRY

1

Focus question

What are the reasons for the military rivalry between the Soviet Union and the United States in the Pacific? How does this rivalry affect the Pacific countries?

▲▲▲ Related questions ▲▲▲

1 What is the rivalry between superpowers and what are its causes?

2 Is there an 'arms race' in the Pacific?

3 How are smaller countries affected by superpower rivalry?

4 What are some alternative ways of reducing this rivalry?

5 What does the word 'security' mean for Pacific Island countries?

6 What is a secure future for the Pacific?

Common assumptions about the Soviet threat

'What are you doing next Sunday?'

'Playing tennis with Sandra. Why?'

'Thought you might like to visit one of those American warships which are coming. They're having an open day, even a navy band. Thought I might take you along if you are interested?'

Karin put down her homework and looked over her shoulder toward her father. He was reading the newspaper and listening to the football. Behind him, through the window she noticed the sky was clear, obviously it was very hot outside. What a bore doing homework she thought.

'Well, do you want to or not? The ship will only be open for inspection tomorrow.'

She paused. 'Why would I want to visit a warship?'

He put down his newspaper and swung around coolly. 'What do they teach you in school these days, eh? The Americans are our allies.'

'Here we go,' she thought to herself.

'We learn about different things these days Dad. Today's wars involve nuclear weapons. Those warships you want to visit also carry nuclear weapons, Tomahawk missiles to be precise.'

Her father walked over to the kitchen and came back with a cold drink. She closed her book and stared at him angrily.

'Kids think differently these days.'

'So you think you know more than your father, eh?'

Karin smiled to herself and turned towards him. 'There are no real threats to Australia these days.'

'What about the Russians? The Soviet Union has warships in the Pacific, that's why we have American warship visits; they keep the Soviets away. You can read about it in the papers.'

'The Soviet Union has not got the ability to invade Australia,' replied Karin.

'So long as the Yanks are there I feel safe. You cannot keep peace without strength.' He sat back, content in his belief.

'Yes, but when you have so many nuclear weapons, like we have today, then nobody is safe. There are almost 60 000 nuclear weapons!' Karin went to her room and came back with a large map showing all the military facilities in the South Pacific. She spread the map out on the table covering his newspaper.

ACTIVITIES

1 Use these questions as the basis for a class discussion.

- **a** How do Karin's views differ from her father's?
- **b** Why has the invention of nuclear weapons changed people's views about using military force to solve problems?
- **c** Some people argue 'if you want peace, prepare for war'. This is also called 'peace through strength'. What is your opinion about these statements?

2 Draw up two columns and list the advantages and disadvantages of foreign nuclear warship visits.

3 Survey another class about their attitudes to nuclear warship visits. Discuss in class what sort of questions you could ask before beginning the survey.

4 Research how many accidents with nuclear submarines and warships have occurred at sea. What were the consequences of these accidents?

Major wars in the region

Since the end of the Second World War the Asia–Pacific region has experienced a number of major wars which have, to some extent, involved either direct or indirect support from the two superpowers: the Soviet Union and the United States. These wars have included those in Korea and Vietnam. In both these wars the United States sent in troops. The Soviet Union has not been directly involved (sending troops) in any Pacific conflict since the Second World War. However, like the United States, the Soviet Union has sent military aid to countries like North Vietnam, to influence the outcome of a war.

The Soviet Union and United States in the Pacific

Both the Soviet Union and the United States are Pacific powers. The United States' Californian coast stretches along the Pacific for 11 059 kilometres while the Soviet Union has Pacific ports in Vladivostok. Both superpowers maintain very large navies in the North Pacific region. There are four main areas of interest which both countries have in the Pacific.

Economic

The amount of trade between the superpowers and the Pacific is an indication of the importance of the region. For example 18 per cent of the imports into Pacific countries come from the United States. The Soviet Union has only limited trade agreements in the Pacific. The Pacific countries are also seen to provide vital trade routes to most important destinations, such as Asia.

Social

The social interest is measured by the interaction between the indigenous people of the Pacific and the superpowers. For example one in four migrants in the United States comes from the Asia–Pacific region. Many of these migrants maintain close family ties. The United States also has direct influence in the life of the Pacific countries through tourism, business and other activities.

The Soviet Union too, has a direct social link with the Pacific, though not to the same extent as the United States. The Soviet merchant fleet and its fishing vessels make visits to the Pacific, including Australia, but apart from official delegations there is limited tourism and interaction. In the past, the Soviet Union has been a fairly closed nation and its main activity in the Pacific has been maintaining its military forces. Mikhail Gorbachev and his introduction of 'glasnost' (openness) and perestroika (restructuring) has led to rapid changes in the Soviet Union, especially its policies in the Pacific. The Soviet Union is seeking closer relations with other Pacific Island countries. It particularly wants to extend its trade, exporting raw materials, including minerals, timber and energy from Siberia.

Military

Both superpowers maintain powerful military forces, including nuclear weapons, in the Pacific. These include land bases, aircraft, troops and ships and submarines. Now that Europe is disarming, the Pacific is perhaps one of the most militarised places on earth. It is also one of the most likely places a nuclear war could start. Since 1982 there has been a rapid increase in the number of nuclear weapons in the Pacific. Added to this, the United States has a policy of placing

Fig. 1 Officers on the deck of a Soviet warship. What effect would a visit by this Soviet warship have on a small Pacific nation?

most of its nuclear weapons on ships and submarines because they believe they are less vulnerable to attack.

Both superpowers test missiles and carry out war games in the region. These war games can include thousands of soldiers, aircraft and many nuclear-capable warships. In the past US warships have carried out simulated attacks on Soviet bases in Vladivostok, coming within kilometres of the Soviet coast. In one incident a Soviet warship rammed an American warship which created international tension. Since the development of more positive relations between the two superpowers these occurrences have been less frequent.

Political

Political interest includes sharing similar views about government, human rights and democratic principles. Both superpowers maintain their system of government is the best, hence each competes with the other in influencing Pacific states. There are contradictions, too, on both sides. For example, the United States holds to democratic principles yet it supported the corrupt dictatorship of Ferdinand Marcos in the Philippines. The Soviet Union supported the Vietnamese occupation of Kampuchea. Influence over Pacific states can be gained through treaties, trade, military support and covert operations which include supporting coups against governments. Because the two superpowers believe their political system is better, smaller countries are often squeezed between them, trying to please both sides to gain better trading relations.

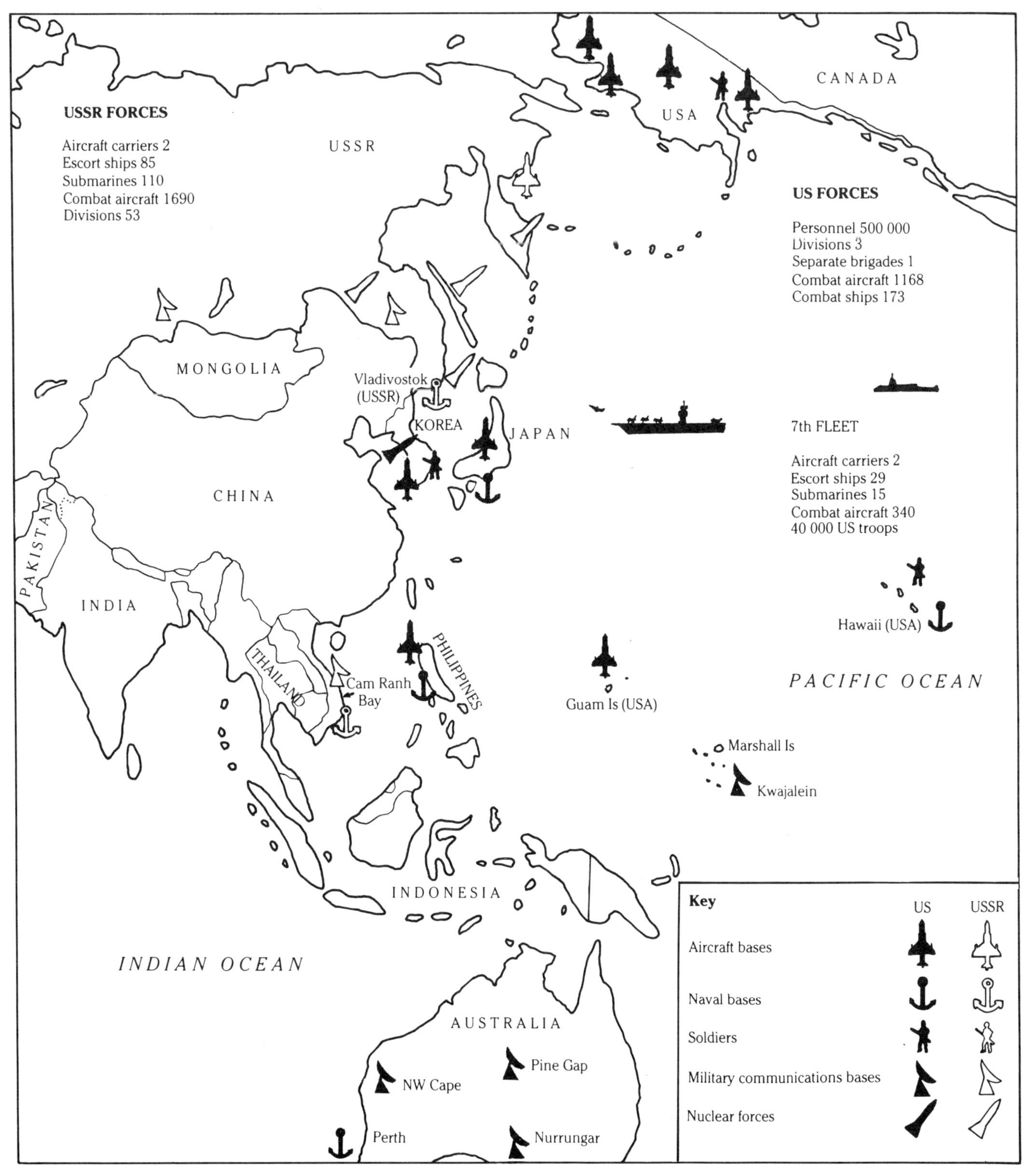

Fig. 2 Military forces in the Pacific. Describe the spread of superpower forces across the Pacific.

ACTIVITY

Can you think of any other areas of interest each superpower would have in the Pacific? List the areas of interest in order of importance and explain why you listed them in this way.

The 'Soviet threat': conflicting views

Read and compare these articles and statements.

Article 1

Pentagon warns Soviet Pacific power growing

By TIM COLEBATCH, Washington, Tuesday

The Soviet military threat to Asia and the Pacific had grown recently with the introduction of newer and more sophisticated warships, planes and missiles to the region, a senior Pentagon official said yesterday.

Rear-Admiral Timothy Wright, the Pentagon's director of international security affairs for East Asia and the Pacific, told a congressional hearing that the buildup had taken place despite a public perception that the threat was lessening.

"I think the Soviet threat has grown, because their equipment capacity has improved, and they've improved the quality of their weapons," Admiral Wright said. "They have increased the projection capacity of their navy.

"They have brought in a new aircraft carrier. They have newer surface vessels, newer submarines. They have increased the capability of their armed forces. They have brought in 1300 aircraft, including fourth-generation fighters."

Admiral Wright said the belief that the Soviet Union was reducing its military presence came from its decision to dismantle its SS-20 intermediate-range nuclear missiles facing China and Japan, its troop withdrawals along the China border, and the reduction of its naval presence in the South Pacific and South-East Asia.

But he said it could direct strategic nuclear missiles and bombs to the same targets formerly covered by the SS-20s. Only 10,000 troops out of 200,000 had been withdrawn from the border region, and its navy was exercising closer to home, probably for budgetary reasons.

Admiral Wright was one of four senior officials appearing before the chairman of the House foreign affairs sub-committee on East Asia and the Pacific, Mr Stephen Solarz, to face a barrage of questions on US policy in the region.

Among other highlights of the hearing:

- Mr Solarz implied that he was considering legislation to cut off US aid to Fiji if its Government adopts a revised constitution which discriminates against the country's Indian minority.
- A senior official said US aid to the South Pacific nations in any case had failed to meet the targets pledged by American officials in regional agreements two years ago.

Mr Thomas Reese, of the Agency for International Development, said this year's aid would be $A17 million, several millions below the amount the US had promised. He blamed Congress for cutting back aid levels generally, noting that US aid to Thailand, Indonesia and India had also suffered.

- Asked which of Indonesia, Malaysia, Singapore, South Korea and Thailand were regarded as democracies, the acting assistant secretary of state, Mr William Clark, replied: "All of them are democratic, but there are degrees of democracy."

The *Age*

Article 2

It is totally inconceivable that the Soviet Union's major surface ships will move into the Pacific and attack Japanese and American warships or cargo ships or sea lanes.

Admiral Naotoshi Sakonjo, December 1982

Article 3

Writing in 1977, Paul Nitze, former US Secretary of the Navy and key strategist in the Reagan Administration, concluded that Soviet submarines and aircraft are not 'cause for serious speculation that the Pacific sea lanes could be severed for any extended period by Soviet naval activities'.

Fig. 3 Victor III Class nuclear-powered attack submarine and an Oscar Class nuclear-powered cruise missile submarine (background). What is the role of these Soviet submarines in the Pacific?

Article 4

Now briefly about the so-called 'Soviet threat' to the South Pacific . . .

We make no secret of our intention to develop relations with the island states . . .

It will depend on what those countries want. If we have expanding trade and economic cooperation with those countries, and growth in tourism, athletic and cultural exchanges, then that will of course mean increased Soviet presence. But in no case will the result be a Soviet military presence.

E. M. Samoteikin, Soviet Ambassador to Australia, 1988

Article 5

In the Pacific as in all other areas of the world, our greatest threat remains the Soviet Union.

Admiral William Crowe, Commander-in-Chief, Pacific, 1985

Article 6

The Soviets are in real trouble in the Pacific. They haven't been able to make much headway ideologically or politically. They have squired some shabby allies — North Korea, Vietnam — whose economies are either stagnant or in decline. At the same time, we are enjoying a better relationship with China than many people anticipated we would. The whole Far East — not just Japan — is becoming the most prosperous market in the world, and the Soviets can't even penetrate it.

Admiral William Crowe, Chairman of the Joint US Chiefs of Staff, News and World Report, 29 July 1986

Activities

1 Write answers to these questions.

a List the statements between those which suggest there is a 'Soviet threat' and those which do not. What evidence is there for each side's arguments? What would you need to know to find out the actual situation?

b After reading the above statements what is your opinion about the 'Soviet threat'?

c How do you think superpower rivalry might affect Pacific Island nations?

d Is there evidence on the television and in the newspapers which suggests both superpowers are looking at each other differently? Find evidence and explain.

e Which of the above statements impresses you most and why?

2 Use this question as the basis for a class discussion.

Ex-President of the United States, Jimmy Carter, once suggested that all the millions of dollars spent on nuclear weapons did not make people feel more secure; most people, especially women, still feel afraid to go out alone at night.

When we talk about security and threats, what are the major threats people are concerned about? Is it, in fact, an invasion from an enemy? Explain.

Soviet and United States military forces

The role of the Soviet Navy in the Pacific is different from the US Navy. United States forces are designed to threaten, attack or occupy foreign lands and control the open seas, a strategy termed 'offensive defence' (military forces which go to the enemy's borders for defence). Soviet forces are primarily devoted to a 'defensive defence' (military forces to defend one's own territory) in the Soviet Far East. Soviet Pacific strategy and military forces are concentrated around what they consider to be the 'American threat'.

The United States has two major bases outside its own territory: the extensive naval facility at Subic Bay, and the Clark Air Force base, both in the Philippines. They also have three major communications bases in Australia: Pine Gap, Nurrungar and North West Cape.

The Soviet Union has large military forces in the Northern Pacific, however, its warships and submarines are not able to extend far beyond Soviet territory. In the past, Pacific nations have been wary of the Soviet Union because it has large military forces, however the Soviet Union is now trying to develop closer economic ties with its Pacific neighbours so that it can find markets for goods and minerals from Siberia. These ties include fishing rights which allow Soviet trawlers to visit Pacific islands to repair and refuel. In particular, the Soviet Union wants to develop economic ties with Japan to sell oil and other raw materials. The Soviet Union now wants to reduce its military spending so more money can be redirected into the domestic market. The Soviet Union has a major naval base in Vladivostok and another, smaller, naval base at Cam Ranh Bay in Vietnam.

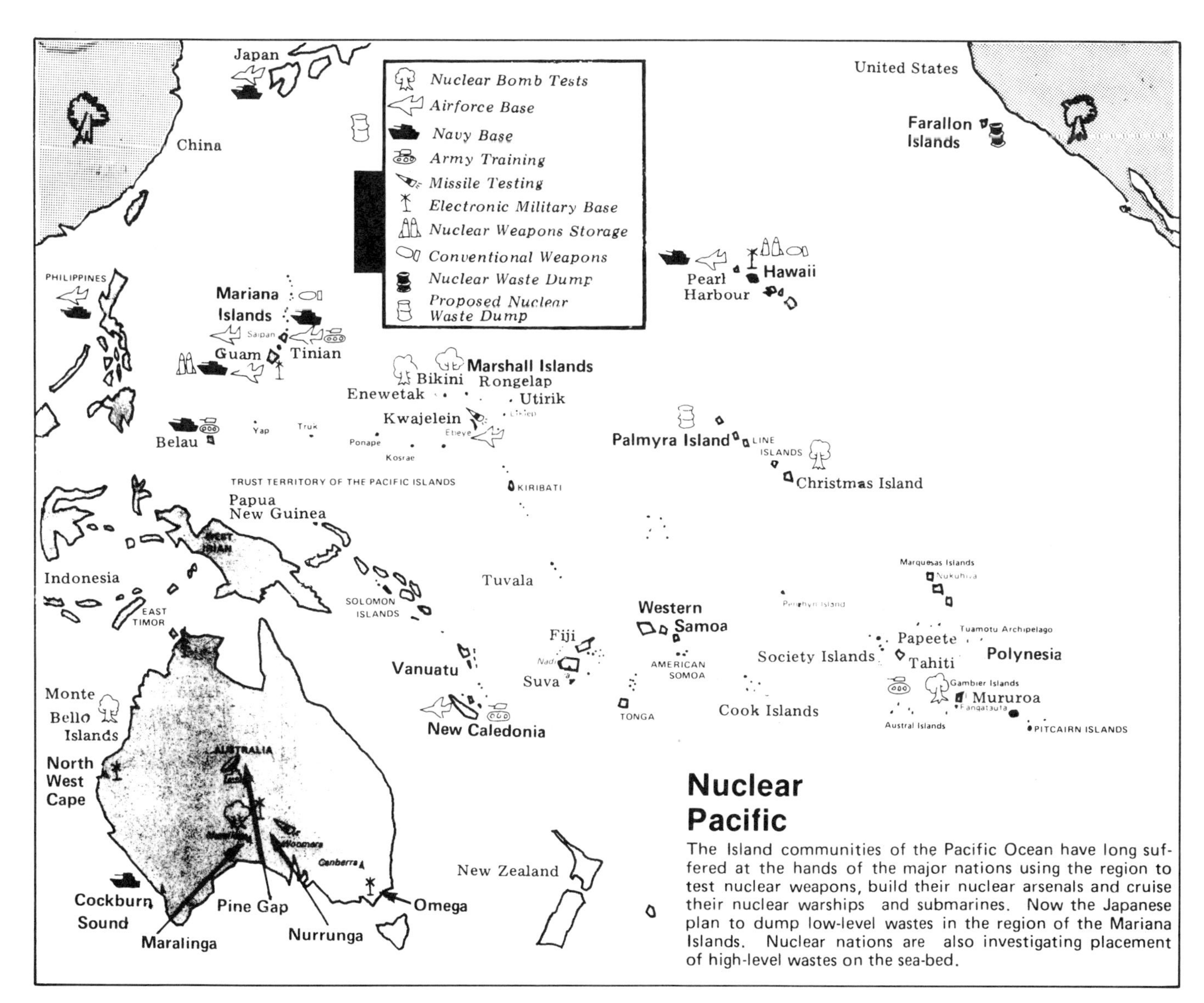

Fig. 4 Soviet and United States nuclear facilities in the Pacific. Do the reasons for using the Pacific as a nuclear waste dump differ from the reasons for using the Pacific for nuclear bases? Why?

ACTIVITY

Examine Fig. 4 and identify the different types of nuclear and military activity which take place in the Pacific and list the countries involved.

- ▲ nuclear weapons testing
- ▲ ICBM missile testing
- ▲ dumping nuclear and other hazardous wastes

▲ possessing nuclear-powered and armed warships
▲ conducting naval exercises
▲ operating bases and other military facilities
▲ mining and exporting uranium

Strategic differences between the United States and the Soviet Union

The United States has naval bases close to the Soviet Union which are warm water ports (do not freeze in winter). The US military forces are even closer to the Soviet Union. For example, in Korea there are over 40 000 US troops and many nuclear weapons. They also have military bases and equipment in Japan. Japan is an ally of the United States and its defence budget is the third largest in the world after the United States and the Soviet Union.

The Soviet Union has a major naval base in Vladivostok but it freezes over four months of the year and locks in naval vessels. However, their naval base in Cam Ranh Bay (Vietnam) is a warm water base and is close to the US military facilities in the Philippines. The Soviet bases are a long way from the United States.

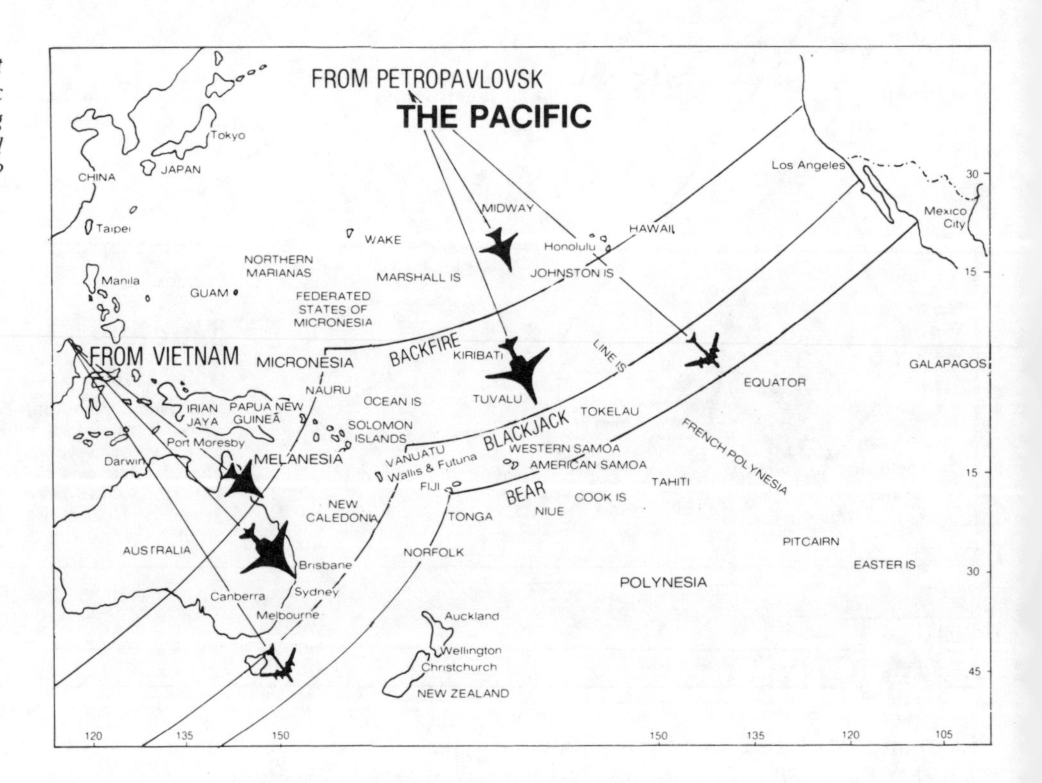

Fig. 5 The range of Soviet aircraft covers much of the South Pacific region. Is this a politically stabilising factor on the region? How do you feel about the 'reach' of these aircraft?

ACTIVITIES

1 Find Vladivostok on your map (Fig. 2).

2 Find the Clark and Subic Bay bases in the Philippines.

3 Find the three US bases in Australia.

4 Write answers to these questions.

a Recently the Soviet leader Mikhail Gorbachev announced that Soviet forces in Cam Ranh Bay (Vietnam) were being pulled back to Soviet territory. Why was this done and what pressure does it put on the United States in the region?

b What advantages does one country have over another if its military and communications bases are closer to the opposition?

Fig. 6 Do you think these warships patrolling the Pacific will always be a part of Pacific life? Why?

Strategic advantage

The Pacific Ocean houses many military facilities. Each side strives for some sort of military advantage. These advantages can include having more weapons, both nuclear and non-nuclear, as well as more ships, planes and submarines. It can mean better technology, well trained troops, friendly allies or natural defences such as being stationed in warm water ports rather than ones which freeze over in winter. But one great advantage is being close to your adversary. The closer you are the more likely it is that you could destroy enemies before they destroy you.

As you can see on the map (see Fig. 2), the US forces are very close to the Soviet Union. Before the Second World War the United States believed it was protected by the vast Pacific Ocean from attack. It was a natural defence. However, after Pearl Harbour, when the Japanese surprise attack destroyed many

American warships, the United States changed its policy and decided to adopt what they call forward defence. That is, being close to the potential enemy and having your forces forward, rather than deployed on your own territory.

The Soviet Union defends its territory by having most of its forces on its own soil (see Fig. 2). Recently the Soviet leader Mikhail Gorbachev announced the withdrawal of military forces from Cam Ranh Bay and the reduction of the number of Soviet submarines and warships patrolling in the Pacific Ocean.

ACTIVITIES

1 Write answers to these questions.

- **a** Which of the two superpowers has the most bases in the Pacific and where are they located?
- **b** Do you think one superpower has a strategic advantage over the other? Why?
- **c** What are the advantages and disadvantages of a Pacific Island nation 'hosting' a foreign military base on its soil?
- **d** What are the advantages for a superpower having a military base on an island?
- **e** Do you think the acquisition of foreign military bases by the superpowers strengthens or weakens security for the Pacific Island countries?

2 Organise the class into two groups in order to debate the question: Does having a stronger military force keep the peace?

Military exercises in the Pacific

The frequency, scope and size of military exercises in the Pacific is growing constantly. For example, 'Team Spirit', a joint exercise involving some 200 000 US and South Korean troops, lasted three months and was the largest exercise in the non-communist world.

In August 1986, US Admiral Lyons, Commander of the US Pacific Fleet, sent a carrier battle group for the first time into the Bering Sea. Pacific fleet ships and submarines are now being sent on unprecedented manoeuvres close to coast-lines.

The Soviets, in their military exercises, have sent jet fighters to penetrate Japan's defence zone in mock attacks, and have held a large scale naval exercise with the North Koreans in the Sea of Japan.

ACTIVITIES

1 Write answers to these questions.

- **a** What are the reasons for these war games taking place?
- **b** In what ways could these war games lead to a conflict, or even war?

2 Use the following situation as the basis for a class discussion.

Imagine one of your neighbouring countries announces it is going to be involved in a large war game which will be a simulated attack on yours. They have given your country another name and they have assured you that it is only a military exercise for their troops.

How would you feel and what would be your response to this action?

Fig. 7 Soldiers on manoeuvres in the Pacific. For what potential purpose might these soldiers be in training?

Case Study 1: Arms race in the Pacific

Read this article and then answer the following questions.

600 N-weapons 'ready in Pacific'

From ANDREW KRUGER of AAP

NEW YORK, Wed. — An American research group has produced evidence that the nuclear-free zone treaty proposed by Australia and endorsed by member-nations of the South Pacific Forum may be too late.

Estimates based on Pentagon documents and other information indicate there are about 600 American and Soviet nuclear weapons already deployed in the Pacific-Asian region at any one time.

According to Nautilus Pacific Action research, a non-profit organisation, more than 2000 nuclear weapons are available for deployment in the region. But, it says, Pentagon procedure manuals suggest that fewer than a third are actually "on station".

Such calculations are imprecise because neither the Soviets nor the U.S. will acknowledge their ships or aircraft carry nuclear weapons.

Nautilus says a nuclear war in the Pacific could result in a two-day exchange of more than 5000 Soviet and U.S. nuclear weapons, or about one tenth of their combined stockpiles.

Targets could stretch from the joint U.S.-Australian communications base at North-West Cape to Japan.

Weapons would include land-based Intercontinental ballistic missiles, nuclear land mines believed buried in Korea, and an assortment of nuclear depth charges, short-range missiles, rockets and artillery shells.

Nautilus made the disclosures to dramatise the 40th anniversary of America's atomic bombing of Hiroshima and Nagasaki.

Previously classified Pentagon documents obtained by Nautilus under the Freedom of Information Act, show that nuclear weapons were stored illegally in Japan from the 1950s to 1966.

Nautilus researcher, Peter Hayes, says: "Newly discovered official documents demonstrate the recklessness and confusion with which the U.S. brandished nuclear weapons in East Asia in the 1950s.

"They also reveal that the U.S. came perilously close to dropping the bomb again in Asia on at least three occasions between 1951 and 1958."

The *Herald*

---

1 Why are so many nuclear weapons stationed in the Pacific and where are they located?

2 Why are Pacific countries concerned about the increasing number of nuclear weapons in the Pacific?

3 What would happen to the Pacific Island nations in the event of a nuclear war in the Pacific. How would these weapons be targeted?

ACTIVITIES

1 Research why the United States considered using nuclear weapons between 1951 and 1958 during the Korean War.

2 Use this question as the basis for a class discussion.

Do you think tensions between the superpowers would be further reduced if they disclosed how many nuclear weapons they had and where they were placed?

Case Study 2: Negotiating fishing rights with the USSR and the USA

Look carefully at the photograph on the next page, read the two articles and then answer the questions following.

Fig. 8 Fees for fishing in the Pacific islands are around $50 000 per year which has led to the building of bigger and more efficient boats. This US fishing boat was seized by the Solomon Islands government. Why would they object to these new hi-tech boats fishing in their waters?

What a fishing accord means for Western allies fighting Soviet influence

From BRUCE LOUDON in Nuku'alofa

THAT was the question being asked last night as American negotiators and their counterparts from 16 South Pacific States — some from among the world's smallest and most insignificant nations — frantically worked to put the finishing touches to a multilateral agreement designed to end the prolonged dispute over the region's fishing rights.

As the meeting closed yesterday a school end-of-term atmosphere erupted. For most of the 40 or so participants in the deliberations, it had been a long, hard slog. More than two years had been spent discussing tuna-fishing arrangements that, without the Soviet encroachment, would have been a simple matter.

But the reality of the Soviet thrust into the South Pacific overshadowed the talks throughout, and that is why, as they were closing last night, the question uppermost in most minds was quite simply this: "Does (the agreement) mean the end of Moscow's drive into the region?"

The answer, alas, is almost certainly "No". For, important as the Nuku'alofa accord will probably be in the affairs of the South Pacific, the agreement is unlikely to turn back the Soviet penetration.

Most analysts say the accord will indeed end a long-standing irritant to better relations between the nations of the South Pacific and the United States. It will improve ties. It may even prompt Washington to show greater concern for the region in other fields, political and military.

But the observers' view is that it will not repel the Soviet tide.

One of the principal American negotiators in Nuku'alofa told The *Australian* last night: "Assuming we have an agreement, it will help our overall relations in the area. But the Soviets have their sights set on the South Pacific, and a fishing agreement is not going to change that."

What was emerging as the Nuku'alofa meetings reached their climax was a clear perception that just an early stage had ended in the contest for the South Pacific.

The *Australian*

Forum steers clear of US-Solomons tuna row

From PAUL ELLERCAMP
in Funafuti, Tuvalu

THE South Pacific Forum nations have held back from taking any retaliatory action against the United States over its tuna-fishing row with the Solomon Islands.

Instead, the forum nations yesterday left the dispute to be resolved in talks between the two countries.

The Australian Prime Minister, Mr Hawke, said there had been no evident support at the meeting yesterday for the Solomon Islands' call for retaliatory trade action against the US.

Mr Hawke said he believed no action should be taken which was not aimed directly at resolving the dispute.

The forum took the decision during the final session of its two-day annual meeting, but it left the wording of a reference to the matter in its communique to a committee consisting of Australia, New Zealand and the Solomon Islands.

It was clear that other States did not want to buy into the row.

On another issue — the dumping of nuclear waste at sea — the forum nations were not so reluctant to distance themselves from the US.

On Monday, the forum decided that individual members should write to the US and Japan to voice opposition to proposals to dump nuclear waste at sea.

Mr Hawke succeeded yesterday in having inserted into the communique a reference which placed the group's decision to work towards a nuclear-free zone in the South Pacific in the context of international disarmament.

The decision on Monday to establish the zone and yesterday's decision to broaden its context are significant for Mr Hawke. They represent valuable weapons when confronted with accusations within the Labor Party that he is not doing enough to further the cause of world disarmament.

Mr Hawke has been at pains to emphasise during the forum meeting the significance of the zone proposal as strengthening the region's commitment to disarmament.

While Mr Hawke recognises that the zone will not stop the French testing nuclear weapons in the Pacific, and it will not stop the arms race, he sees it as a significant demonstration of international will on these issues.

Not only did the forum nations accept Australia's proposal that a working group be set up to develop the zone concept, but they also tacitly endorsed the draft set of principles to govern the zone which Australia put forward before the meeting.

The forum set the working party a target date of 1985 to receive a draft treaty to put the nuclear-free zone into effect.

Under the draft principles, the zone would ban the acquisition, storage, manufacture and testing of nuclear weapons within the South Pacific region. (One of the tasks facing the working group is to define precisely the geographical limits of the zone.)

The dumping of nuclear waste would also be banned.

Nevertheless, it is difficult to see how the zone could prevent the Japanese or the Americans dumping waste if they were determined to do so. Mr Hawke has already acknowledged that it will not stop the French testing nuclear weapons.

The forum communique issued last night also dealt with progress by the French Government towards independence in New Caledonia, describing it as much too slow.

During the debate on New Caledonia on Monday, a number of States urged that the planned date for a referendum on independence should be brought forward from 1989 to as early as 1986.

Following another intervention from Australia, the forum also recognised the sincerity of the French Government in wanting to grant New Caledonia independence.

The *Australian*

1 Is the United States justified in its arguments against the Soviet Union using fishing facilities in the islands?

2 What do the Soviets want?

3 What are the main concerns for the Pacific Island nations?

4 How does the agreement address the problems of all the nations involved?

5 If Kiribati accepted Soviet fishing vessels into its ports, could this affect its relationship with the United States? How?

6 What are the circumstances which led to the Solomon Islands government finally seizing an American tuna boat?

7 The situation was described as 'the mouse that roared'. What problems develop for a smaller nation, totally dependent on fishing as its main export, when faced with an uncooperative superpower?

8 How effective was the Solomon Islands action outlined in the second article? Explain the risks involved.

9 How could the Americans respond to the Solomon Islands' action?

ACTIVITIES

1 Discuss in class the problems smaller island nations face in looking after their own interests when dealing with the two superpowers in the Pacific region.

2 What are the options?

You are the Prime Minister of a small, Pacific Island country totally dependent on your fishing industry. You are told that a superpower is sending in huge fishing trawlers which will clean up most of the fish in your area. You are on friendly terms with this country and they provide you with aid and technology and other services. You have signed an international treaty which says that you own the water 200 miles from your shores. Although every other nation has signed this treaty, the superpower does not recognise it so they intend to fish close to your shores. They argue the fish are in international waters.

What can you do?

Option 1
Allow the foreign trawlers to come in and fish without protest. (If yes go to Option 3; if no go to Option 2.)

Option 2
Send a message saying the trawlers are in your territory and refuse permission for them to fish. (If yes go to Option 6; if no go to Option 3.)

Option 3
If the trawlers came in they are likely to severely reduce the amount of fish left in the area and thus reduce your export earnings. This would put you in direct conflict with your country's major industry and employer, the fishing companies. It could also make you an unpopular leader with people accusing you of being weak and it could lead to your defeat in the next elections.

The fishing companies announce they will send out their own trawlers and break the nets of the foreign ships. Do you support this action? (If yes go to Option 5; if no go to Option 4.)

Option 4

You have decided not to support the fishing companies. They withdraw financial support from your government and other members of your party openly criticise you. Large demonstrations outside parliament are organised. Economists predict that the loss of export income from fish taken by foreign trawlers will cause unemployment and severe problems. Your days as Prime Minister are numbered.

Option 5

You are trying to please both parties. The foreign country will probably continue its aid to your government but the internal pressure and your inability to stand up to the foreign trawlers will probably cause your downfall. You have to decide which comes first; the interests of your country as an independent nation able to support itself by exporting fish or a partially independent nation reliant on overseas aid which is supplemented by exporting fish.

Option 6

You have decided to send a strong protest note saying that any foreign trawler fishing in your country's territory without a permit will be seized. You also instruct your nation's fishing fleet to go out and protest. You have instructed your small navy of two patrol boats to seize any foreign trawler taking fish in your territory. The foreign trawlers ignore your letter and begin fishing within the 200 mile off-shore zone. The foreign power says it will cut off all aid and services and refuse to import fish if any of its trawlers are seized. What do you do? Back down from your position (go to Option 3) or decide to seize a foreign trawler which is in your territory (go to Option 7)?

Option 7

There is a news flash around the world that a foreign trawler was seized by a small Pacific Island nation. You have been instructed to return the vessel immediately or there will be serious economic consequences. Other countries in the world support your action. Another major power announces it will sign a fishing treaty with you. There are large demonstrations in the street supporting you. You negotiate a special trade agreement and the superpower accepts your arguments.

3 List all the issues for both countries and identify possible solutions.

4 As a class write down what you believe an international treaty, such as the one discussed above, should contain. How could it be enforced?

Case Study 3: New Zealand bans nuclear-armed and powered warships

Fig. 9 Protests against nuclear armed ships continue but their success has been minimal. Why do these protests continue?

In 1985, the New Zealand government introduced a ban on any nuclear-powered or armed warship entering its ports. Because the United States has a policy which does not either confirm or deny whether its warships carry nuclear weapons, the New Zealand government banned them.

Read this article and answer the following questions.

NZ brings in its nuclear ship bans

Wellington, Thursday

New Zealand became officially nuclear-free today with Parliament passing legislation enshrining the Lange Government's ban on nuclear-powered and nuclear-armed warships and aircraft.

The New Zealand Nuclear Free Zone, Disarmament and Arms Control Act formalises a policy which forced the end of Wellington's 35-year-old Anzus alliance with Washington last year.

It was passed on party lines.

In a sometimes rowdy debate the Prime Minister, Mr David Lange, who is expected to call a general election in August, described the act as a "watershed" and a "turning point".

He said New Zealand in the past had used its defence budget as a "subscription to some sort of nuclear ancillary club".

"This Government is proud that for the first time in 40 years New Zealand has made a fundamental reassessment of what constitutes our security," Mr Lange said, adding that nuclear weapons were irrelevant and detrimental to his country's defence.

In past months, the opposition National Party has described the legislation as the "anti-Anzus bill" and has committed itself to a return to port visits and the Western alliance.

Today the opposition leader, Mr Jim Bolger, told the single-chamber Parliament the bill was composed of "half measures and contradictions" from the "looney left" and that the implementation of a non-nuclear policy had made Mr Lange the "toast of Moscow".

Earlier, at a news conference, Mr Bolger compared the act with the appeasement policies of Britain under Neville Chamberlain prior to World War II.

Introduced in December 1985, the relatively slow passage of the bill coincided with a rapid deterioration in US-New Zealand relations.

By August last year Washington had withdrawn its defence guarantee for New Zealand, leaving Wellington out of defence exercises, with little intelligence sharing and no special rights to arms and equipment sales.

Apart from banning the deployment, testing and storage of nuclear devices and waste, the bill prohibits port visits by nuclear-powered ships. Additionally the Prime Minister can grant foreign warships and military aircraft permission to enter New Zealand waters and airspace only if he is satisfied they are not carrying nuclear weapons.

According to the United States and Britain, this provision cuts across their global policy of neither confirming nor denying the existence of nuclear weapons on individual vessels.

The ban on nuclear warships came into force with the July 1984 election of the Lange Labor Government, but was not put to the test until February 1985 when the nuclear-capable USS Buchanan was refused permission to visit.

The *Age*

---

1 Why has New Zealand banned nuclear warships?

2 How has the United States responded to New Zealand's position? Explain how each superpower would view the decision and why.

3 Do you think New Zealand is at risk of invasion by not being in the Anzus Alliance? Explain.

ACTIVITIES

1 Research the debate concerning New Zealand's banning of nuclear-capable warships. What has been Australia's response? What other countries have similar bans and why?

2 Do you think New Zealand's decision to ban nuclear warships reduces or increases the arms race and the likelihood of nuclear war? Prepare a written response which refers to Mr Lange's comments.

Case Study 4: Mururoa and the first French nuclear tests

By the beginning of July 1966, after three years of intense preparations, the Mururoa testing-base in French Polynesia was operational. The first nuclear bomb was placed on a barge anchored in the lagoon and detonated. The result was a catastrophe. All the water contained in the shallow reef basin was sucked up into the air before it rained down, covering all islets with heaps of radioactive fish and clams, whose slowly rotting flesh continued to stink for weeks.

The continued testing by France of nuclear weapons began to affect a range of countries. Radiation laboratories in Australia and New Zealand continued to register increases of nuclear material, especially in milk, in their own countries

Fig. 10 The Greenpeace ship Rainbow Warrior *was bombed by French secret agents in NZ. What role does Greenpeace play in the Pacific to highlight the arms race?*

Fig. 11 Nuclear explosion on a Pacific atoll. Why was the Pacific chosen for nuclear weapons testing?

and throughout the Pacific Islands. More and more civic associations, church groups and political parties, ecological groups and trade unions began putting pressure on France to cease testing nuclear weapons in the South Pacific. The protest was followed by a nationwide boycott of French goods, airlines and shipping companies. The mail service to and from France was halted by Australian and New Zealand postal workers. Little by little these protests and boycotts spread to other Pacific countries.

In May 1973, Australia and New Zealand instituted proceedings in the International Court of Justice in the Hague against France on the grounds that the fallout from the French tests at Mururoa had polluted their national territories. France countered by refusing to recognise the competence of the International Court of Justice in defence matters. The World Court decided that radioactive pollution across national boundaries was not a defence matter but a health matter and in June ordered France to cease all nuclear testing until the case was closed.

It became obvious the French government was going to ignore the ruling and so the new Prime Minister of New Zealand, Norman Kirk, took the unprecedented step of sending a warship to Mururoa with a cabinet Minister and the press on board. Other citizens also took boats into the test area, including Greenpeace. This annoyed the French who delayed the tests, and it attracted international attention to the issue. But after postponing the tests for six weeks French commando units boarded the yachts, seized their crews and impounded their yachts. Eventually, however, France agreed not to conduct atmospheric tests and to do all their future testing underground. Since 1966, France has exploded 157 nuclear bombs in the Pacific.

Read the articles on the next page, and then answer the following questions.

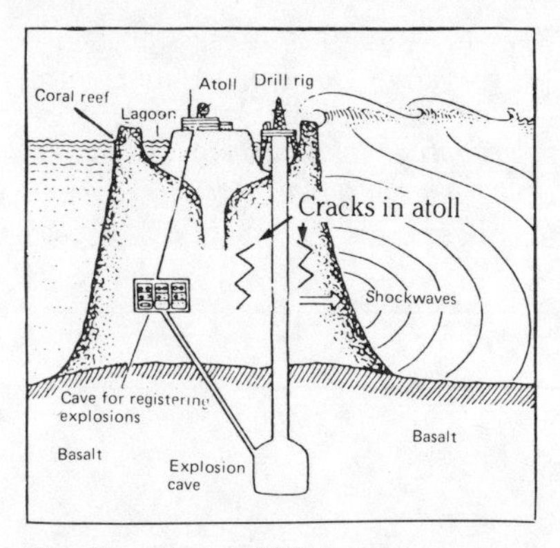

Fig. 12 Since 1974 French nuclear explosions have been carried out underground. These have cracked Mururoa Atoll. What dangers are posed by continuing nuclear testing at Mururoa?

Article 1

The first effect [of French (underground and atmospheric) testing at Mururoa] would be the contamination of the plankton, that's the layer of living material which produces about 50% of the world's oxygen and also provides food for the fish, so after the contamination of the plankton you have a lower oxygen supply and you'd also have to check the food chain because all this material eventually will come back to the dinner table. I would imagine some of the biggest impact, even from the weapon testings in the 1950s and 1960s will be in the 1990s or the year 2000, so it's still out there in the ocean coming back through the food chain.

Interview with Dr Rosalie Bertell, cancer research scientist in the effects of low level radiation on ABC Radio's 'Background Briefing', 28 August 1983.

Article 2

1 Testing is essential to the credibility of our deterrence as I have just said, particularly to keep pace with technological breakthroughs and counter measures.
2 Our testing is innocuous and you will notice that we are the only country that lets a scientific team check on the testing and we are ready to accept other teams of that nature to our testing grounds.
3 Mururoa is as French as Hawaii is American and I could take other examples close to home.

From a speech by Mr Claude Berlioz, First Secretary, French Embassy, Australia, at the first National Conference on Unionism and Peace, Adelaide, 1987.

1 List the long- and short-term effects of the French nuclear weapons testing program in the Pacific region.

2 What has been the French attitude towards countries and groups which are calling for a stop to the tests?

3 What are the main problems involved in underground testing at Mururoa?

4 Do you think that the French should still be testing in the South Pacific? Give reasons for your answer.

ACTIVITIES

1 Draw a diagram showing your understanding of how the plutonium and other contaminated materials get into the food chain and so into our food.

2 Write a letter to the French Embassy giving your views on France's nuclear weapons' testing program in the Pacific.

3 Investigate the groups such as the Nuclear Free and Independent Pacific (NFIP) organisation which have opposed French nuclear testing and list their main reasons why it should cease.

Case Study 5: Nuclear Free Zone (NFZ)

Many island countries are concerned about the increasing nuclearisation in the Pacific. Over a seventeen year period France, the United States and Great Britain have exploded over 250 atomic and thermo-nuclear bombs. France still tests nuclear bombs in the Pacific at Mururoa. These tests had, and still have, tragic consequences for the Pacific region.

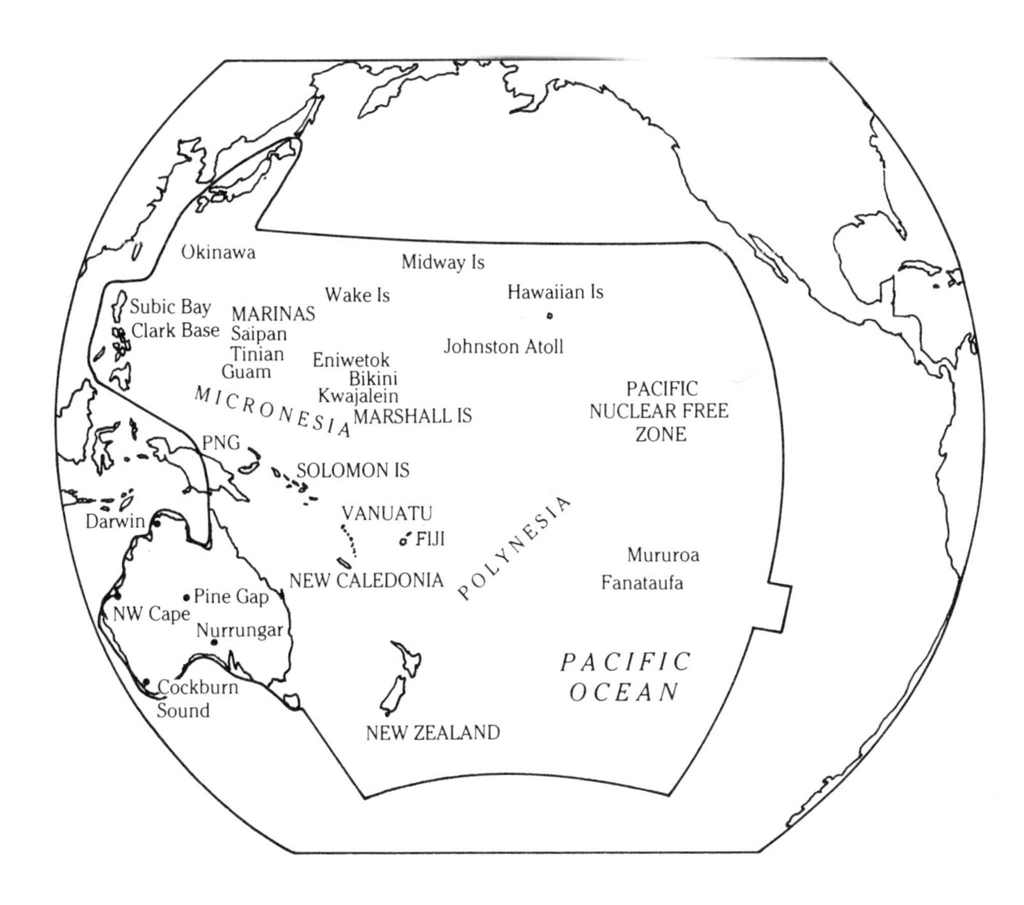

Fig. 13 The Nuclear Free Zone in the Pacific was proposed in 1980 at the Nuclear-Free Pacific Conference. Do you think NFZs reduce the risk of nuclear war? Why/why not?

The Pacific nations are not only concerned about nuclear testing, waste dumping and upgrading of nuclear facilities for new and more powerful weapons, but they have come together and tried to establish the Pacific as a Nuclear Free Zone (NFZ) under the Treaty of Rarotonga. This proposal emerged as a consequence of the Australian Government's opposition to French nuclear testing at Mururoa. China and the Soviet Union have signed the Treaty; the United States, Britain and France have not.

Read the article on the next page and then answer the following questions.

Forum agrees on PM's N-free plan

From MICHELLE GRATTAN, chief political correspondent

FUNAFUTI, 27 Aug. — South Pacific countries yesterday agreed to an Australian set of draft principles for a nuclear-free zone.

The principles allow for each country to make its own decision about visiting nuclear ships and imply, although they do not explicitly spell out, the right of ships carrying nuclear weapons to sail through the zone.

Australia is to chair a working party on the details. It is hoped this can produce a draft treaty for the zone, which would be considered at next year's forum.

A move by New Zealand to have the zone proposal put to the United Nations General Assembly later this year failed. Other countries believed that the countries of the region needed to do more work before the proposal formally went to the United Nations.

Mr Hawke, at a Press conference after the decision, strongly contested the suggestion that a nuclear-free zone which allowed the transit of vessels with nuclear weapons would be meaningless.

"No country which enters into a treaty concept of this kind does so on the basis that it is giving away its right to make decisions which are relevant in its perspective to its own strategic considerations," he said.

"We are not living in cloud cuckooland; we are living in a world in which the Soviet Union has extended its power considerably," Mr Hawke said.

It was illogical to imply a country could not have a view about what was necessary for its strategic relationships but at the same time want to limit the operation of other elements of the nuclear fuel cycle in the region, he said.

The decision on the Australian draft principles is a victory for the Hawke Government and, although the zone would have limited real meaning, it adds further to the Government's credentials on the disarmament issue, which it has taken up vigorously.

The principles the 13 forum nations adopted yesterday declare that:

- There should be no use, testing or stationing of nuclear explosive devices in the South Pacific.
- No South Pacific country will develop or manufacture, or receive from others, or acquire or test any nuclear explosive device.
- There should be a prohibition on the dumping and storage of nuclear waste in the South Pacific.
- South Pacific countries reaffirm their sovereign rights to decide for themselves, consistent with the objectives of the zone, the security arrangements and such questions as access to their ports and airfields by vessels and aircraft of other countries.

The *Age*

1 Briefly, outline what the Treaty of Rarotonga states.

2 What do you think the Pacific nations are trying to gain from the Treaty with France, USA and the USSR?

3 Examine the American response to the Nuclear Free Zone proposal and identify their concerns.

4 Why do you think the Soviet Union and China have signed the Treaty but France, Britain and the United States have not?

5 What are the strengths and weaknesses of the Treaty? List advantages and disadvantages for the Pacific Island countries?

6 Do you think this is a positive step to reduce superpower rivalry in the Pacific? Some Pacific countries will not sign it because they believe it does not go far enough.

ACTIVITIES

1 How do the concerns of the Pacific nations differ from those of the United States, Britain and France in relation to signing the NFZ Treaty?

2 Divide the class into various groups representing the different Pacific countries and the United States, the Soviet Union, France, China and Britain.

As a class, brainstorm all the issues which you think are involved in writing a Nuclear Free Zone Treaty. Then, in your own groups, represent your country's issues and concerns, and try to negotiate a treaty which will satisfy each country and at the same time have a strong nuclear-free position.

3 Research another treaty in which various nations have come together to seek common agreement. What are some of the main problems with international treaties?

Case Study 6: Missile testing

Look at Fig. 14, read the information following, and then answer the questions.

Fig. 14 Missile test ranges in the Pacific used by the USSR and the USA. Is there any safe haven in the Pacific?

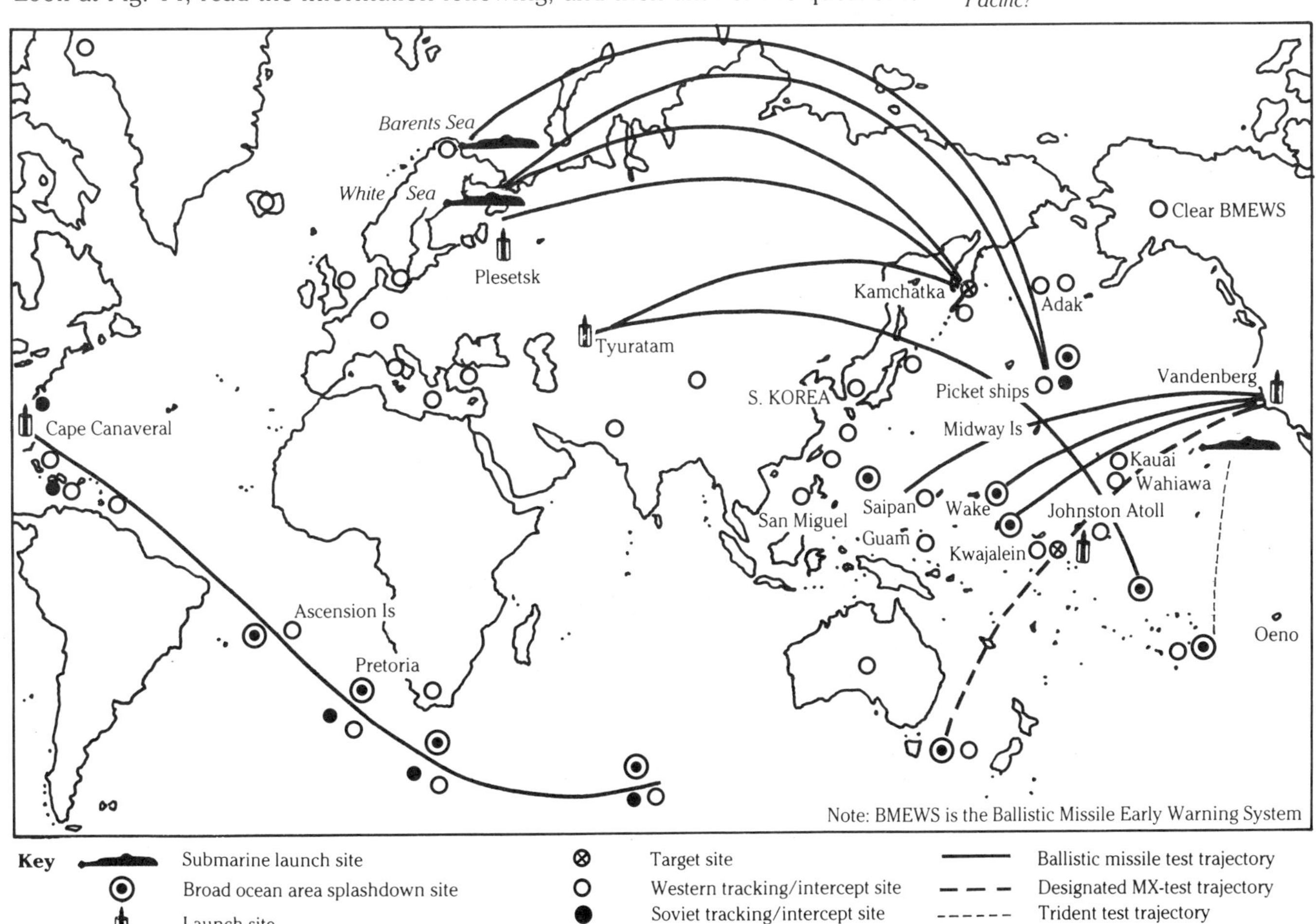

Since 1989 both the United States and the Soviet Union have been conducting long-range missile tests into the Pacific. Missiles are fired from Vandenberg Military base in California to Kwajalein in the Marshall Islands. The Soviets fire their Intercontinental Ballistic Missiles (ICBMs) from Plesetsk, in Soviet Europe, into the central Pacific region (see Fig. 14). The Soviet Union does not have a land base for its missiles tests but relies on 'Picket Ships' which are stationed around the impact sites.

1 On Fig. 14 locate where both superpowers launch their missiles and the Pacific countries where they land.

2 List the ways in which these missile tests directly and indirectly affect the Pacific Island nations.

3 What are some of the ways Pacific countries can protest against missile testing?

4 Design a protest banner against nuclear missile testing. What issues would you highlight?

ACTIVITIES

1 Write a feature article for a newspaper which discusses the following statement.

Banning missile tests would slow down the arms race but reduce the ability of a country to defend itself.

2 Write answers to these questions.

a After examining the case studies, which actions do you think reduce the rivalry between the two superpowers? Why?
b Apart from building up their navies and military forces, what other options do the superpowers have to reduce rivalry and establish a lasting peace in the Pacific?
c How can the concerns of the superpowers be met to achieve 'common security'?

RESEARCH PROJECTS

1 How can the Pacific Island nations protect their own small industries and, at the same time, maintain a friendly relationship with either superpower?

2 How do the needs of the Pacific nations differ from those of the superpowers?

3 Examine American and Soviet military policies and their effect in the Pacific.

4 Given the changes taking place around the world and the movement towards more peaceful relations between the two superpowers, what sort of changes should occur in the future to ensure a safer Pacific region, and what can you do as an individual to bring this about?

5 Explain the controversy over the burning of chemical weapons by the United States on Johnston Atoll.

Resources

Barnett, J. & McLaurin, R. *US Defense Posture in the Pacific*, United States Information Agency, 1987.
Dalton, L. *The Nuclear Environment*, Movement Against Uranium Mining, Friends of the Earth, 1983.
Danielson, B. *Poison Reign*, Penguin, Ringwood, 1985.
Department of Defense. *Soviet Military Power, 1986*, Department of Defense, United States Government US Printing Office, Washington, 1986.
Dibb, P. *The Soviet Union as a Pacific Power*, working paper no. 81, Research School of Pacific Studies, ANU, Canberra, 1984.
Fahey, S., Peake, M. & Quanchi, M. *The South Pacific*, Victorian Ministry of Education, 1989.
Firth, J. *Nuclear Playground*, Allen & Unwin, Sydney, 1987.
Fry, G. *A Nuclear-Free Zone for the Southwest Pacific: Prospects and Significance*, working paper no. 75, Research School of Pacific Studies, ANU, Canberra, 1983.
Hayes, P., Zarsky, L. & Waldon, B. *American Lake: Nuclear Peril in the Pacific*, Penguin, Ringwood, 1986.
Military Publishing House, *Whence the Threat to Peace*, Novosti Press Agency Publishing House, Moscow, 1987.
Scientific Research Council on Peace and Disarmament, *Pacific Ocean Security*, Nauka Publishers, Moscow, 1987.
Thakur, R. & Thayer, C. *The Soviet Union as an Asian Superpower*, Westview Press, Macmillan, Australia, 1987.
White, R. *The New Zealand Nuclear Ship Ban: Is Compromise Possible?* working paper no. 30, Research School of Pacific Studies, ANU, Canberra, 1988.

2 The Marshall Islands

Focus question

What have been the effects of nuclear testing in the Marshall Islands?

▲▲▲ Related questions ▲▲▲

1. Why do countries test nuclear weapons in the Pacific?
2. What sort of effect do you think the nuclear weapons tests have had on the environment?
3. How do you think nuclear weapons testing affects the indigenous population?
4. What are the current problems in places where nuclear weapons have been tested?
5. What can be done to improve the future of people affected by nuclear weapons tests?

Fig. 15 Children playing in the sand on the Marshall Islands. Are they aware of the global situation and their role in world military strategies?

Children of the sand

The children were trying to catch a white and blue crab near the shore. It ran sideways, avoiding their laughing and taunting as they prodded it with sticks. Further out in the ocean warships pitted the horizon.

Behind the rows of palm trees, along the long white sandy beach, men and women were sitting together, trying to get used to their temporary home on the new island. They were not happy because the fishing on the new island was poor and there was a lack of fresh water. The coral reefs were too shallow for good fishing. The men and women wanted to go back as soon as possible. They were also tired of the sailors and the scientists who kept giving them chewing gum and sweets whenever they complained about the conditions. They had agreed to move because they were told the experiments were going to benefit many people.

At 6.45 a.m. there was a blinding flash of light followed by a fireball of intense heat. Tens of millions of degrees, shooting upward at a rate of 500 kilometres per hour. The children stood staring at the huge swirling cloud of fire. The crab slipped away into the clear water.

The islanders imagined their homes being blown apart. Hundreds of millions of tonnes of material from the reef, island and lagoons were lifted up into the air. The islanders watched as the enormous cloud of smoke and debris rose into the sky. They wept as their island became engulfed in fire.

Three to four hours later they noticed a 'gritty' white ash falling over the water and moving toward the island. Soon, all the sixty-four people on the island became covered in the white ash. One of the twenty-eight servicemen on the island reported, 'If you can imagine a snow storm, that's what it's like'.

The dust and ash formed a 51 cm thick layer on the island. The drinking water turned brackish and yellow. The airforce men asked to be evacuated immediately but were told there were no planes available. By nightfall, people began to experience severe vomiting and diarrhoea.

ACTIVITIES

1 Look at the endpaper map and locate the Marshall Islands.

2 From the information provided, outline in point form what you think is happening. What is the 'white dust'?

3 Discuss in class why you think the Islanders moved. Do you believe they knew what was going to happen?

Nuclear weapons testing in the Pacific

Fig. 16 These 44 gallon drums advised people not to proceed down this road near Maralinga, Australia. Were the Australian government and people well advised and prepared for this testing by the British?

How many of us stop to think about how and where nuclear weapons are tested and the effects these tests have on people. Since 1945, there have been over 250 nuclear weapons tested in the Pacific. The countries involved have been the United States, Britain and France. Most of the tests were carried out by the United States between 1946 and 1960. Nuclear weapons tests were conducted in the Marshall Islands and on Enwetok and Bikini Atolls. Because of world protests about the danger of nuclear weapons testing and the deadly effects of fallout, the United States and the Soviet Union agreed to conduct all weapons tests underground after 1963.

France continued to conduct atmospheric tests on Mururoa Atoll, in French Polynesia, until 1975 when intense international pressure forced them to carry out further testing underground. Australia was involved in nuclear testing programs between 1952 and 1962 when the British carried out tests in South Australia at Maralinga, Emu Field and Monte Bello off the coast of Western Australia. Even though countries now conduct tests underground radioactive material still leaks into the oceans and underground water tables which eventually gets into the food chain.

Fallout effects of nuclear testing

1 A nuclear bomb explodes and tiny particles from the bomb mix with the soil.

2 Hot ashes and fine particles rise into the air to form a huge cloud.

3 The ashes and particles spread out and begin to fall back to earth as radioactive fallout. Some particles are carried by high winds into the upper parts of the atmosphere.

4 The ashes and particles that have fallen on the ground travel slowly down into the soil over many years.

5 Radioactive particles may then enter plants through roots and end up in the food. The same process affects fish.

6 When people eat radioactive food they take in radioactive particles that stay in their bodies.

7 Radioactive plutonium is dangerous for 250 000 years. This is called its 'half-life'.

8 Radiation contamination can cause lung and thyroid cancer, leukaemia, birth defects and other illnesses.

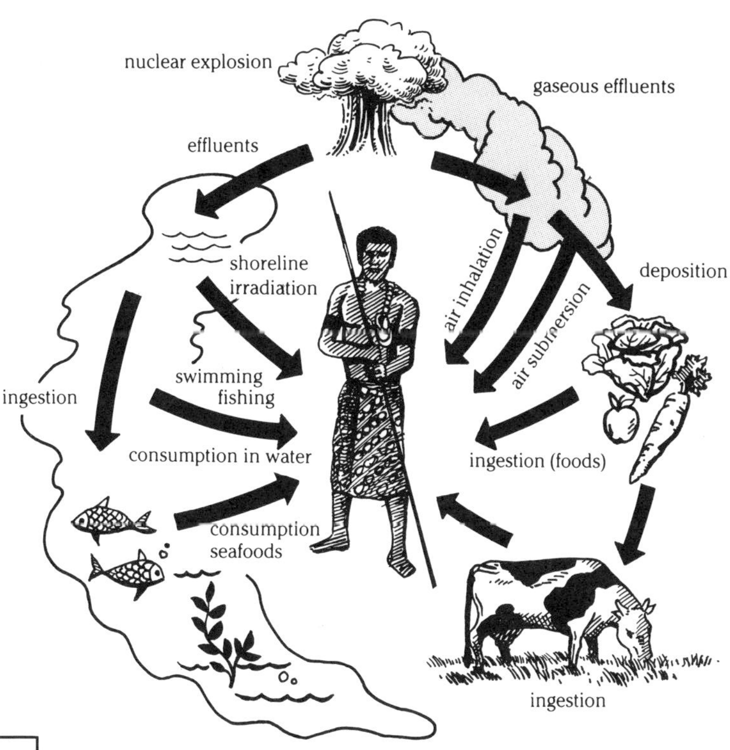

Fig. 17 How does radiation get into our food supply?

ACTIVITIES

1 Write answers to these questions.

a What is fallout?
b What happens to fallout once it gets into the atmosphere and oceans?
c Why is fallout so dangerous?
d Explain how plutonium gets into the food chain.
e Find out what 'half life' means.
f How does radiation affect the body?

2 The first atomic bomb was dropped on Hiroshima. Investigate the effects of radiation poisoning on the citizens who survived.

Why test nuclear weapons?

Ever since the first atomic bombs were dropped on the Japanese cities of Hiroshima and Nagasaki in 1945, both the United States and the Soviet Union have been engaged in a massive arms race to produce bigger and more deadly missiles with increased accuracy.

The first nuclear weapon was the atomic bomb, the next major weapon was the hydrogen bomb which is nearly one thousand times more powerful than the Hiroshima bomb. All these new nuclear bombs and missiles have to be tested somewhere. The United States, France and Britain chose the Pacific to test their first nuclear weapons.

In 1988, this arms race began to ease in the northern hemisphere as the United States and the Soviet Union signed agreements on dismantling and destroying short-range nuclear weapons in Europe. The Peace Movements in both countries have played a significant role in bringing the dangers and costs of the arms race to public attention. However, in the Pacific, the arms race remains.

ACTIVITIES

1 Research and identify all the countries which have tested nuclear weapons. Where have these tests been conducted? Plot them on a map, listing the number of tests per country. Also list the countries which are currently developing or could have nuclear weapons.

2 Write answers to these questions.

a Why do you think so many weapons were tested in the Pacific region? Give five reasons.

b What environmental problems occur with nuclear weapons testing?

c Who gains most when nuclear weapons are tested?

3 Discuss in class whether or not nuclear weapons testing increases the arms race.

4 Do the following group activity. A decision has been made to declare a desert near your town a nuclear test site. You have been advised that it is perfectly safe, although on days when tests are conducted, you will need to keep your windows closed. More jobs and services are promised and the local council is seriously considering the new proposal. Your class represents the local residents. This is what some of the interested parties believe:

Builders: will get more work

Hospital: concerned about the effects on children

Police: will need a larger force to protect area

Bank: more money for the local town as people invest

Real Estate: house prices will go up or even down

School teachers: concerned about the effects on children

Peace group: totally opposed because of dangers

Farmers: concerned about their cattle and milk being contaminated

Mothers: worried about effects on their children and during pregnancy

Church: wants assurances that the tests will not cause harm

Local business: means more income and expansion with more people

Students: don't trust it

What are the main issues and what would you decide? Class members can role-play the interested parties and represent their particular opinions.

The Marshall Islands

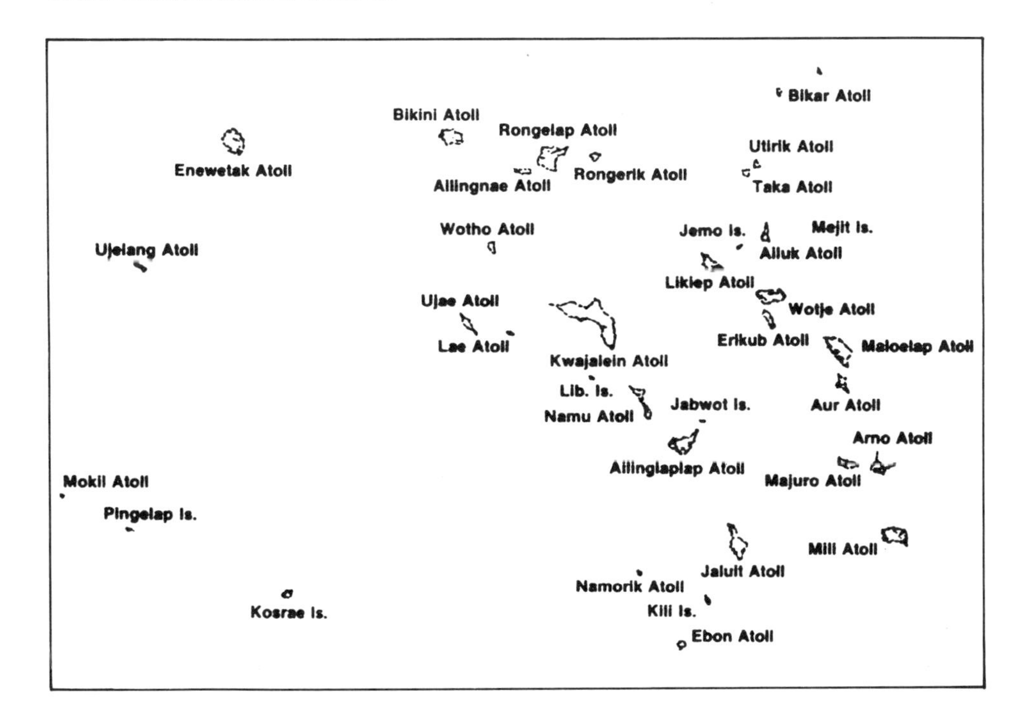

Fig. 18 The Marshall Islands comprise 29 atolls and 4 single islands. What impact does this geographical structure have on the ability of the Marshallese to undertake group action against the testing?

Look at the endpaper map and at Fig. 18 and identify the area of Micronesia and the following islands and atolls.

▲ Bikini Atoll
▲ Eniwetok
▲ Kwajalein
▲ Ujelang
▲ Rongerik
▲ Utirik
▲ Majuro (capital of the Marshall Islands)
▲ Rongalap

ACTIVITIES

1 Look at the maps and consider the geographic area of the Marshall Islands.

a Calculate the distance between Bikini Atoll and your city.

b Calculate the distance between Rongelap and Kwajalein.

c What is the distance from the eastern-most point to the western-most island atoll?

2 What are some of the problems associated with living on small islands with great distances between them? These problems could be associated with the location of services like transport, education, employment, hospitals, industry, banks, airports and government.

Background brief

The Marshall Islands are at the eastern edge of Micronesia, approximately 3200 kilometres west of Hawaii, and consist of 1152 low coral islands and islets totalling only about 180 square kilometres in area. Almost all these atolls are small, some no more than coral outcrops dotted with coconut palms. They are scattered across a vast expanse of ocean.

Fig. 19 An atoll in the Pacific. How does the geography of this atoll leave it open to destructive natural elements?

The Marshallese have a single language with two dialects. The ancestors of today's Marshallese population of almost 33 000 were expert out-rigger builders, navigators and sailors. They travelled widely from their small, self-sufficient communities and, to this day, have strong ties with the neighbouring islands of Kiribati, Nauru, Ponape and Truk.

The tradition of landowning is an important feature of Marshallese society. This is related to their lineage and kinship system and to the political and economic relations among individuals and groups.

The four foreign rulers in the Marshall Islands

Spain

Spain maintained some control of Western Micronesia from late 1600. Traders and missionaries were well established throughout most of Micronesia by the late 1800s. (American missionaries, traders and whalers also began to arrive at this time.)

Germany

Germany declared protection over the Marshall Islands in 1885 and bought the rest of Micronesia from Spain in 1899 for $4.5 million.

Japan

At the outbreak of the First World War (1914–1918), Japan took control of the entire area now known as the Pacific Trust Territory. After the war ended, Japan developed extensive economic activities which attracted large Japanese communities. By 1938 almost 58 per cent of Micronesia's population was made up of settlers from Japan and Korea. It was from Micronesia that Japan launched its surprise attack on Pearl Harbour in 1942 which started the Pacific War between Japan and the United States.

United States

The United States captured the islands from the Japanese at the end of the Second World War (1939–1945) in fierce battles which cost the lives of more than 5000 Micronesians. The United States continued to administer the Marshall Islands and other districts under a United Nations agreement called the Strategic Trust until 1983. Under the conditions of the trust, the United States was permitted strategic and military use of the area. The United States was also obliged:

▲ to guide the territory towards self-government or independence
▲ to promote the economic advancement and self-sufficiency of the inhabitants
▲ to promote their health
▲ to protect them against loss of their lands and resources

Under this Trust Territory arrangement the United States decided to test nuclear weapons on Bikini and Eniwetok Atolls in Micronesia.

ACTIVITY

Research in what ways colonial powers who occupied nations in the Pacific directly changed their culture. Investigate how the Marshall Islands changed under American control.

Testing begins

In 1945 the United States began to search for a nuclear test site.

Article 1

> [Their requirements included] a site within control of the USA, uninhabited or subject to evacuation without necessary hardship on large numbers of inhabitants . . . offering a protected anchorage at least six miles in diameter.
>
> *US Department of Energy (DOE), 1983*

Article 2

> The Seabees [naval carpenters] built a model village on Rongerik that anyone would be proud to live in. The natives are delighted, enthusiastic about the atomic bomb, which has already brought them prosperity and a new promising future.
>
> *US Navy press statement, 1946*

In 1946, one month after the decision was made in Washington to use Bikini Atoll for nuclear weapons testing, the US Military Governor told King Juda, leader of the Bikini Islands, that the United States wanted to test nuclear weapons 'for the good of mankind and to end all wars'.

The Americans said that Bikini would be returned to its people at the conclusion of the tests. The Bikinians believed their move was only temporary and so they agreed to relocate. They resettled on nearby Rongerik Atoll, 206 kilometres east of Bikini. There were poor quality coconuts, unusable well water and many species of fish which were poisonous on Rongerik. It was not an ideal location for the local Marshallese who had prospered on Bikini Atoll.

Once the Bikinians were removed from their island, the US navy burnt down the remaining huts and began preparation for what was to be the United States largest nuclear blast, 'Bravo', which was later detonated on Bikini Atoll.

ACTIVITIES

1 Write answers to these questions.

- **a** Why did the United States choose Bikini Atoll as a place to test nuclear weapons?
- **b** What do you think was the attitude of the United States to the Marshall Islanders?
- **c** What is a 'Trust Territory'?
- **d** How did the United States convince the Marshallese to relocate?
- **e** What sort of impression does the navy press statement give?

2 Organise yourselves into three groups representing the Marshallese, the military, and representatives of the United Nations in order to role-play the first meeting to discuss the proposed testing.

Group one represents the Marshall Islanders who have lived peacefully on Bikini Atoll for hundreds of years. This group can organise themselves into a small village with each member playing a particular role. Select a leader and some elders who would represent the views of the villagers. The Marshall Islanders are Christian and quite trusting of their visitors. The group should adopt a welcoming and trusting role although they are insistent that their move will only be temporary. However, there are some in the community who do not want to move because they do not fully trust the American military officers. They also know there are few fish at the new location and that the lagoons are not fresh. There are also fewer coconuts and other foods.

Group two represents the United States navy who want to test nuclear weapons on Bikini Atoll. This group's job is to work out how they can convince the Bikinians to leave their island so testing can begin. They will make every effort including giving the children chewing gum, the young people radios and the promise of new and modern houses on the new island where the Islanders will be relocated. They also assure the Islanders that they will be provided with food until they move back to Bikini Atoll.

Group three represents the United Nations and must ensure that the conditions of the trusteeship outlined on p. 35 are maintained. They want to protect the Marshallese but also recognise the United States military claims.

Each group can decide on and then present their main arguments. Identify the strengths and weaknesses of each party's position. What other options were available for the Bikinians and the United States? How would you have dealt with this issue today?

Conflicting reports

After the 'Bravo' test there were conflicting reports of serious radioactive contamination.

Article 1

During the course of a routine atomic test in the Marshall Islands, 28 United States personnel and 236 residents were transported from neighbouring atolls to Kwajalein Island according to a plan as a precautionary measure. These individuals were unexpectedly exposed to some radioactivity. There were no burns. All were reported well. After the completion of the atomic tests, the natives will be returned to their homes.

US Atomic Energy Commission (AEC) press release following the 'Bravo' blast 1954 (The AEC was responsible for the tests.)

Article 2

When we arrived on Kwajalein we started getting burns all over our bodies and people were feeling dizzy and weak. After two days something appeared under my fingernails and then my fingernails came off and my fingers bled. We all had burns on our ears, shoulders, necks and feet and our eyes were very sore.

Etry Enos, Pacific Islander on Rongelap who suffered contamination

After three months of examinations and treatment at the United States military base at Kwajalein, the Rongelap people were resettled temporarily on Egit Island in Majuro Atoll because of high radiation levels on their return to Rongelap.

Article 3

Well before receiving your letter I was concerned about the fate of the Polynesian [Pacific] people . . . those who declare that these tests are not dangerous are liars!

Dr Albert Schweitzer, Nobel Peace Prize winner, famous philosopher and physician writing in 1964 to a friend in Tahiti, John Teariki

ACTIVITIES

1 Imagine you are a journalist who has received the above articles on the telex machine. Write a short article for the newspaper reporting this event.

2 You are a member of a United Nations team responsible for the welfare of the Marshallese. You have received the above information and you intend to investigate the reports. What would you do to find out the truth and what problems may arise in your investigation?

3 Write answers to these questions.

a From the above articles, piece together what you think happened on Bikini Atoll.
b Why would the United States Atomic Energy Commission try to cover up any serious contamination if it did occur?
c Do you think all the dangers involved in these tests were properly considered?
d Explain how the Islanders' concerns were dealt with.

4 Copy Fig. 18 and colour the listed islands, which were contaminated by radioactive fallout from the 'Bravo' test, in red.

Bikini	Rongerik	Jemo
Allingnae	Taka	Mejit
Ailuk	Wothje	Rongelap
Bikar	Utirik	Mejato
Likiep		

Then, using Bikini as the central point, draw a circle around the above islands which were contaminated by radioactivity from the 'Bravo' test.

5 Use these questions as the basis of a class discussion.

a How far did the fallout spread? Give its diameter.
b What sort of warning was given to the Islanders when they were sent to Rongerik?
c What precautions could have been used to prevent the contamination?
d What are the long-term effects of these tests on Bikini Atoll and on the inhabitants?

Resettlement 1954

Soon after the 'Bravo' test it was considered safe for the people of Rongelap to return to their island. However, the number of still-births and miscarriages rose by more than 100 per cent in the first four years following their return.

The United States responded to a petition by the Bikini Islanders to stop the testing and to be returned to their islands.

Article 1

It is the conviction of the United States that it has the responsibility not only to its people but to all the peoples of the free world to maintain at a maximum its capacity to deter aggression and preserve peace. Thus it believes that . . . further tests are . . . absolutely necessary for the eventual well being of all the people of this world.

US Statement to the United Nations Trusteeship Council, 1956

Article 2

Even though . . . the radioactive contamination of Rongelap Island is considered perfectly safe for human habitation, the levels of activity are higher than those found in other inhabited locations in the world. The habitation of these people on the island will afford most valuable ecological radiation data on human beings.

Brookhaven National Laboratory Report on Rongelap and Utirik

Article 3

Several of my babies, who were healthy at the time they were born, died before they were a year old . . . Altogether I lost four babies. My son Winston, was born just one year after the bomb and he has had two operations on his throat for thyroid cancer.

Minji Kel, Utirik Atoll, 1958

ACTIVITIES

1 Write answers to these questions.

- **a** What are the reasons the United States gave for rejecting the petition and what are the main arguments they use for continuing their nuclear testing program? Give your evaluation of these reasons.
- **b** How can you account for the different stories given in Articles 2 and 3?
- **c** List the ways in which the Marshallese have been affected by the testing.

2 Poetry is a powerful way of expressing how people feel. Write your own poem which expresses what you think about nuclear testing in general.

3 Write a response which expresses your own opinion of this statement: The United States has fulfilled its obligation under the 'Trust' agreement with the United Nations.

The fate of the Marshall Islanders and resettlement today

In 1983 the United Nations Trusteeship was effectively terminated when the Marshallese signed a Compact of Free Association with the United States. This Compact officially gave them independence, however, they are still dependent on economic aid and the agreement allows the US to continue using the islands for military purposes. For example MX missile and Star Wars testing continues on Kwajalein.

Fig. 20 The US military has taken over a large part of Kwajalein Atoll. What impact would this have on the traditional life and economy of the island?

Fig. 21 Ebeye in the Marshall Islands — one of the most crowded places on earth.

Since testing nuclear weapons in the Pacific began, and in particular on the Marshall Islands, indigenous peoples have been resettled for long periods of time. Even in 1990, many of the Islanders have been unable to return to their pre-1947 homes. Most young Marshallese have never been to their pre-nuclear testing island homes.

Fig. 22 Overcrowding on Ebeye. Describe what life would be like living on Ebeye. Where would you work or grow food? How would you survive?

Ebeye is an island of a mere 74 acres where over 8000 Marshallese live. Most of the people who live there have been resettled from their native islands in order to make way for a splashdown site for testing Intercontinental Ballistic Missiles (ICBMs) fired from California to Kwajalein. Their poor living conditions are in stark contrast to the American military who live and work on the nearby Kwajalein military base.

Fig. 23 (Below left) Living conditions on Ebeye. Why do the houses look so poor when the US military spends so much in this region?

Fig. 24 US military facilities on the Marshall Islands. Compare this photograph with Fig. 23.

In 1978 a Trust Territory study, *Ebeye Redevelopment, Gugeegue and Carlson Development* revealed serious public health problems. It stated that:

▲ 8000 people live on 74 acres
▲ most of the housing is substandard and deteriorating
▲ 36 per cent of the work force is unemployed
▲ more than 50 per cent of the people are under the age of fourteen
▲ the electrical power plant system 'is severely limited and results in numerous breakdowns'

Even today little has improved on Ebeye.

ACTIVITIES

1 Examine the pictures of Ebeye carefully and identify what sort of social problems would occur from this overcrowding.

2 As a resident on Ebeye, you have called a meeting of local citizens to try and improve the conditions on your island. In small groups write up an action plan which you will present to the United States military authorities. Once this is finished decide how you would implement this action plan.

3 During the last decade the United States has shown reluctance to hand over millions of dollars in aid to Belau, another Micronesian territory until it takes out the anti-nuclear clause in its constitution. Considering the Marshallese experience, discuss why the people of nearby Belau are opposed to military bases and nuclear weapons. Outline what their arguments might be.

Fig. 25 Food aid has made the once subsistence Islanders dependent on the United States. Examine Fig. 20 again and describe the relationship between the two pictures.

Pacific 'biological time bomb'

U.S. nuclear testing blamed for birth defects

By DAVID E. ANDERSON
UPI Religion Writer

VANCOUVER, British Columbia — Darlene Keju-Johnson looked steadily at the 900 delegates of the World Council of Churches.

The delegates, as they listened attentively, often squirmed in their chairs or looked away as the young woman, a native of the Marshall Islands, described the young infants born to her friends, infants who die in a matter of hours.

"The Marshallese describe these babies as 'jellyfish,' " Johnson said. "The baby is born on the labor table, and it breathes and moves up and down, but it is not shaped like a human being. It looks like a bag of jelly."

"Sometimes, babies are born with growths like horns on their heads, while others have six fingers or toes."

These births, she told the sixth assembly of the World Council of Churches, are the result of U.S. atomic and nuclear weapons testing, testing that has been going on since the early 1950s.

Johnson spoke at a special plenary session of the council on problems of the indigenous people of the Pacific islands.

Among all the rhetoric, the theology, the cries from the poor and the oppressed, the people of the Pacific, in their dry, understated way, made one of the most dramatic presentations to the delegates from the 300 member communions around the world.

A kind of deep anger and resentment runs through many of the people — an anger directed at the United States, which they blame not only for causing the problems in the first place but also for providing inadequate medical treatment for those who do suffer as a result of the U.S. nuclear testing program.

In 30 years, she said, U.S. scientists "have never provided the Marshallese with personal medical records or tried to explain their health problems to them."

"This is why the Marshallese are today requesting the help and support of doctors internationally who are independent of the U.S. government to provide the necessary health care treatment and monitoring programs that the Marshallese so urgently need."

She also said the United States has over and over again relocated the Marshallese, most recently forcing hundreds of people living on Kwajalein to live on the tiny 66-acre island of Ebeye which now houses 8000 people.

She said the medical facilities for the natives are grossly inadequate and the island has been called a "biological time bomb," but that the Marshallese are denied treatment just three miles away at the U.S. installation.

"It is time we, the Marshallese people, controlled our islands," she said. "There is growing resentment against the military presence at Kwajalein and it is only a matter of time before we remove the base," she said.

The *Sunday Star-Bulletin and Advertiser* (Honolulu)

4 Try and identify some of the short-term and long-term solutions to the problems faced by the Marshallese in re-establishing their pre-nuclear lifestyle.

5 What are the United States responsibilities for bringing about better human rights policies for the Marshallese?

6 It is argued that if the tests had not been carried out on Bikini Atoll the Americans would not have been able to develop nuclear weapons which have prevented a major war breaking out between the superpowers: the Bikinians took the brunt of it but this is better than an unsafe world. What do you think?

RESEARCH PROJECTS

1 Sione left school at the age of twelve. He is unemployed and spends most of his time with other friends playing video games, watching television and videos, drinking and playing cards. Now he receives regular welfare payments from the United States. Most of the food he eats is 'junk' food imported from the US. There are no jobs, except for a few on the American military bases and there is little prospect of him getting a job. He has never been to Bikini though his parents often tell him how life was so much better before the Americans came and tested their nuclear weapons on their atoll. He knows none of his family traditions. He does not respect his elders anymore and he feels society has no place for him. He no longer has a role. Drinking is one form of relief from his situation.

a In what ways can Sione's personal, community and cultural situation be improved?

b Examine other countries which experienced nuclear weapons testing. What were the effects of these tests?

2 In 1952 Australia agreed to allow the British to test atmospheric nuclear weapons in South Australia. A special Royal Commission was ordered when it was discovered that Aboriginals had suffered death and miscarriages well after the tests were concluded. What were the results of this investigation? Can any comparison be made between the Aboriginals and the Marshallese?

3 Write an essay which discusses in what ways the United States fulfilled or did not fulfil its obligations under the United Nations Trust Territory agreement.

Resources

Anglim, J. *Palau's Strategic Position Places Palauan Democracy at Risk*, working paper no. 40, Research School of Pacific Studies, ANU, Canberra, 1988.

Dalton, L. *The Nuclear Environment*, Movement Against Uranium Mining, Friends of the Earth, Melbourne, 1983.

Fahey, S., Peake, M. & Quanchi, M. *The South Pacific*, Victorian Ministry of Education, Melbourne, 1989.

Gale, R. W. *The Americanisation of Micronesia: A Study of the Consolidation of U.S. Rule in the Pacific*, University Press of America, Washington, 1979.

Marshall Islands: A Chronology 1944–1983. Micronesian Support Centre, Honolulu, Hawaii, 1983.

Nuclear Free Independent Pacific Co-ordinating Committee, *A Peaceful Pacific*, Nuclear Free and Independent Pacific, Sydney, 1985.

Siwatibau, S. & Williams, D. *A Call to a New Exodus*, Lotu Pasifica Productions, Fiji, 1982.

Vitarelli, W. *Micronesia as Strategic Colony: The Impact of US Foreign Policy on Micronesian Health and Culture*, Culture Survival Inc., Cambridge MA, 1984.

World Council of Churches Delegation to the Marshall Islands, 20 May–4 June, 1983. *Marshall Islands: 37 Years Later*. Commission of the Churches on International Affairs, World Council of Churches, Vancouver, 1983.

Living with Change

3

Focus question

How has the introduction of Western society affected the traditional culture in the Pacific?

Fig. 26 Traditional produce and craft markets were a way of life on most Pacific islands.

Fig. 27 The development of modern shops and the importing of foods has had an impact on life in the Pacific. Describe this impact.

▲▲▲ Related questions ▲▲▲

1 Compare the differences between the traditional Pacific lifestyle and that of Europeans.

2 In what ways did Europeans introduce industry and change?

3 What effect has Western influence had on Pacific Island culture?

4 How have these changes put pressure on traditional culture?

Case study 1: Lopeti and Konnai (Part One)

Each day Lopeti took his out-rigger canoe into the lagoon and fished. Often he took in four or five large fish and some clams after a morning's work. Sometimes he collected rock crabs. Other men from his lineage worked with him. The island held three clans, each of which had enough land to sustain their respective families.

Lopeti married Konnai and moved into her clan. In his culture family must come first and he was bound by a set of well defined obligations to his own kin. One of his obligations was to support his wife's family. He was expected to contribute free labour to his wife's lineage and to help with the many other tasks that the group carried out including providing food and using any of his special skills. He had to do as his wife's brothers or any other senior member of his wife's lineage asked. This sometimes put Lopeti under considerable pressure.

The food he caught was always shared with the rest of the family or lineage. Sometimes he would barter for certain goods from another clan but money was never used; goods were the currency. On top of this Lopeti had to undertake any jobs given to him by the Chief and they could be long and time-consuming. Life on the island was not as free and easy as people presume because each person has responsibility and a role to play in this community.

Fig. 28 A traditional local village in the Pacific. How would this lifestyle change with western intervention?

Because of his knowledge of the local fishing areas Lopeti was invited to apply for a new job funded by an Aid agency. The new project was to increase the amount of fishing so the island could export fish to another country and earn export revenue. The new government job meant Lopeti was bringing home a fortnightly pay check rather than a string of fish or armfuls of clams from the ocean.

Fig. 29 Preparing fish for export. Who would be the end consumers of these fish?

Now that Lopeti's days were spent either in the office or doing field work it limited the time he could spend with his kin. However, despite the new job, his obligations to the kin did not change although, as a government employee, he is obliged to offer his services to any and all who seek them regardless of their traditional relationship to him.

His responsibilities now extended beyond the kin to all people who have an interest in the fishing project. His kin can demand other sorts of obligations which can include some of his salary, a bigger share of the aid project or securing a member of his kin in employment if another job arises. In fact, what his new government job was doing was increasing the number of groups who can and will make demands on him.

Case study 2: a student

I went to New Zealand to get qualifications and then came home when my mother became sick. I got the School Certificate, University Entrance, and then went to work in the New Zealand Post Office. I passed all the exams and held several positions of responsibility in big post offices before I came back, even though I was only thirty-two. I got a job in the post office in Apia without trouble, but when I went for promotion I missed and another girl, whom I knew, got it. The second time I went for promotion I missed to that girl again. My cousin worked in the Public Service Commission then and so when I told her about it, she checked the girl's record and

> she hadn't got anything like my qualifications. I was talking about that when I heard from someone else that she is related to a man who is on the committee that looks after the promotions . . . I decided to come back to New Zealand . . . I knew I couldn't win . . . unless you play it that way . . .
>
> *From* Mobility and Identity in the Island Pacific *(see 'Resources')*

Case study 3: a government worker

A young Samoan man had been persuaded to return to Western Samoa to run a government enterprise, but resigned to take another position in the private sector. This is his account:

> One problem was that the local elite had been used to treating the venture as their own personal preserve. Every week I got calls from people wanting me to place relatives, or lend equipment for their private use. They were really put out when I refused, because they seemed to regard that as one of the perks and probably used to it [before] to show people that they were big numbers in town . . . I complained to various people, but no action was taken.
>
> *From* Mobility and Identity in the Island Pacific *(see 'Resources')*

ACTIVITIES

1 Examine these conflicting obligations.

A As a government employee Lopeti must offer his services and official responsibilities to all people who want them regardless of their kin. He can allocate his salary as he chooses but his official work is to serve the whole community. He cannot use all his resources to merely serve his own kin. His supervisors could fire him or even impose pay deductions and other penalties if he is seen to be using his position to favour his kin.

B On the other hand, for failing to provide for kin and others to whom he is especially obligated, he can also come under difficulty. If he does not provide to the satisfaction of the kin, he can undergo the humiliation of being looked on as being mean and stingy and then suffer loss of status among the kin and the humiliation of his wife.

Divide into groups and try to answer the following questions.

a What were the additional demands placed on Lopeti once he began his new job?
b What must the fisherman do to satisfy both obligations?
c What changes occurred between his old role and new role?
d How can the aid project actually break down traditional roles and values?
e What do the three case studies have in common? What are the options for Islanders returning with qualifications and experience into the traditional kinship culture?

2 Do you know of any other cultures where these social conflicts occur? Investigate another example and make a comparison with the one above.

Case study 1: Lopeti and Konnai (Part Two)

The kin lived together and were made up of four families. They ate from what they jointly produced. Even the children were raised in their kin group. In short, the lineage group worked as a single unit because they prepared food together, shared the child rearing, ate together and built houses and other shelter together. The food was prepared in a single cookhouse which symbolised the friendship and unity of this social group.

After the first two years of paid work three other members of Lopeti's kin became employed in other jobs which were created by the money earned from exporting the fish. Earning money gave them some independence from the rest of the kin even though they fulfilled their obligations. Lopeti kept his wage rather than handing it over to the Chief.

Fig. 30 How have supermarkets changed both eating habits and lifestyles on Pacific islands?

As time went on, the paid income earners bought food from the new stores and they became less dependent on the other members of the lineage for food and other goods. This meant that families could eat when they wanted and the food was not shared. This led to more cookhouses where families prepared their own food. This in turn meant that less local food was produced because couples went to the food stores which contained imported food and so the tasks of looking after the garden and fishing declined. Soon Lopeti was buying tinned fish from Japan.

As the head of the lineage lost control over the economy and supervision of the garden and food, so too did he begin to lose his authority in the lineage. Added to this, the couples began to take more responsibility over their own children's education which reduced the role of the senior members of the lineage. Lopeti also wanted to decide to which school he was going to send his children, a decision previously made by the lineage seniors. With his increased income Lopeti and other families began to buy their own land.

Fig. 31 The type of traditional housing found on many Pacific islands. Describe how it is constructed. How does it suit the climate of the region?

Fig. 32 Compare the traditional housing with these new apartments in New Caledonia. Which do you prefer and why? Which do you think the native population prefer and why?

ACTIVITIES

1 In point form, list the events which led to the Chief having virtually no authority in his kin.

2 Write answers to these questions.

a How has the role of the senior members changed?

b What are the advantages and disadvantages of these changes for the families?

- **c** How has the cash economy (using money rather than barter and sharing responsibilities) changed traditional culture?
- **d** Why would Lopeti buy a tin of fish from Japan rather than go out and fish in his out-rigger?
- **e** How would these changes affect the role of women in society?

3 Discuss in class how traditional kinship differs from that in your own cultures.

4 Working in groups or pairs select one Pacific Island and make a thorough investigation of its culture including its religion, customs, marriage, roles of males and females, trade and authority. How does it compare with your cultures? Prepare a presentation for the class.

Traditional roles in society

Traditionally, in Lopeti's kin, the males and females had specific roles in the lineage. The women were expected to care for the children, weave baskets, and perform household chores including food preparation. Men were involved in building houses, and constructing canoes involved in inter-island warfare. Men and women engaged in fishing and growing vegetables. Everyone had their own roles to play and each participated in a complementary manner to the well-being of the marriage. Women also played a significant role behind the scenes when land or other goods were distributed. While women were not Chiefs or held titles, nevertheless they were powerful figures in the decision-making.

Fig. 33 Women working in Fiji. Carefully examine the vegetation in the background. Can you identify any plants? What sort of produce do you think the women are processing?

Both males and females were taught to respect each other. But although women did not enjoy equality with men, they were often protected by family members if poor treatment was dealt out.

War between the sexes

Read these two poems.

Women and Housework

Work, work, work,
I am tired
Of marriage.
He bosses me:
Do this,
Do that.
He thinks I am
A machine,
There's always plenty to do.

He is inconsiderate;
I wish he was a woman
To taste work.

Work, work, work,
I am exhausted.
I loved the family
It is everything
To me.

But when in high spirits
He steps out and calls:
'Shut up!'
Please pass my love,
I am not what he thinks.

Lemu Darcy

Working Mother

My children don't know me:
They call me Jully not 'Mummy'.
They see me,
Two hours before bedtime,
An hour in the mornings,
No time for a cuddle, or play;
No time to feed, bathe or clothe them —
Just a peck on the cheek and,
'Bye bye, be good!
See you at four.'
I'm never at home during the week —
Too busy making money.
The only times I see them
They are asleep in bed..
I spend the night alone
Reading;
They spend their days alone
With the house-girl.
My children don't know me.

Jully Sipolo

Fig. 34 How is the role of women changing?

Fig. 35 How do quick changes in women's roles create conflict in traditional society?

A CTIVITY

Use these questions as the basis for a class discussion.

a What do these poems tell us about the status of some women in the Pacific? Can you find similarities in your own country?

b In what ways has the new role of women become more difficult?

The problems of development

What kind of changes has modernisation caused in the Pacific Islands? In the first place it has caused an upheaval in men's traditional roles. There is increased dependence on store-bought food items and so it is common today to see young men, who in the past would have been fishing, picking breadfruit or working in the farms, now loitering in the town without anything to do.

Fig. 36 Changing roles in society have left many men feeling alienated and without a place in the community. What changes have occurred?

Their traditional warfare has been replaced with rival gang fighting and their role of builder has been taken over by skilled carpenters, masons and tradesmen now using imported materials. However, their sisters are still occupied with much the same household chores that they always performed.

The inactivity and freedom that young men experience today often brings with it feelings of pain and insecurity. Stripped of their former roles in the community, many young men no longer enjoy the satisfaction of knowing that they are making a genuine contribution to their family and kin. The dislocation that they experience may be identified to some extent in the high rates of delinquency, alcohol abuse and juvenile arrests.

ACTIVITIES

1 Write answers to these questions.

- **a** What are the key issues the women are raising in their poems?
- **b** In the two poems it appears family relationships and responsibilities are breaking down. Why is this occurring?
- **c** How has modernism affected males in the Pacific Islands?
- **d** Is it impossible to go back to the past? What could be done to reduce the types of conflicts that have arisen in the present?
- **e** What has been the effect of giving aid for 'development'?

2 Select one Aid agency. Research the different types of aid given to poorer nations. Which do you consider to be most beneficial and why? How can we provide aid without necessarily changing the culture of the receiving nation?

3 Do the following group activity. Organise yourselves into three groups representing a traditional kin, a government department, and the rest of the kins on a Pacific island.

Group 1 represents the kin with three traditional families living in a shared and cooperative lifestyle. A son and a daughter from the kin are employed by the government to work with the whole island community. The kin expects the son and daughter, who are now working in a government department, to use their new influence and position to help them.

Group 2 represents a government department which organises fishing exports on a small island and employs the son and daughter in their project. The department wants all the community to benefit from the project. The department understands the problem of dealing fairly with each kin and expects their new employees to divide the resources equally among them.

Group 3 represents the other kins who also want to support and benefit from the new government project. They feel annoyed that their family members were not employed so they intend to watch carefully to see how the resources are shared.

A new tractor has been purchased by the government department. The different kins all want to use it. The government employees must decide how the tractor will be used. However, they are caught between their obligation to their kin which expects the tractor first, and the other kins. Each group should present their point of view and then the three groups should try and come to some agreement which satisfies everyone. Once the role-play is finished, spend some time discussing in class how easy or difficult it was to reach such an agreement.

The effects of a cash economy

Fig. 37 Bartering: simple exchanges without a currency. How does western intervention change this?

The village community was self-sufficient and independent. The Islanders existed on fishing, plants and some local trading (bartering) with other island communities. When the Europeans came they introduced a cash economy; instead of bartering they paid money and rather than acknowledging the tradition of inheriting land from elders, the Europeans bought and sold it.

ACTIVITIES

1 If you introduced a car to an island you would need the following: roads, signs, spare parts, petrol stations, traffic police, facilities to import materials, bridges and repair facilities. Can you think of any more?

In groups of three, write down all the extra items, materials and services (infrastructure) you would need for:

- ▲ electric power
- ▲ an airport
- ▲ skilled labour
- ▲ a hospital
- ▲ telephone

a How would the car alter the economic structure in a village community?

b What happens to a Pacific Island culture when a cash economy is introduced? What are the advantages and disadvantages of it?

c How has the cash economy affected the traditional gender roles?

2 Discuss in class in what ways the Islanders can benefit from both their own and Western cultures.

3 Why are most Pacific Island nations in debt? Select one nation as a case study. Research its main industry and to whom it owes money. Present your findings as a report to the rest of the class.

Other impacts on traditional culture

Fig. 38 With western influence also comes gambling and other social ills. Should this be prevented? How? Why?

In American Samoa, television was established to 'provide compulsory universal education to school-aged children . . . and to rapidly acculturate them into American society and patterns of life'. Added to this, television had an obligation to 'conserve the best of Samoan culture'. In 1962, when funding was approved to set up television in American Samoa, there were to be no entertainment programs apart from 'travelogues, or 30 minutes of old film or something else'.

Ten years later the education programs were drastically reduced and the three channels now screen 178 hours a week of entertainment programs direct from America. The local ten hours is made up of church, sport and a fifteen minute agricultural program which is usually about North America. Ninety-three per cent of the population in American Samoa has access to television. Of the 1000 video titles available in Western Samoa a high percentage depicts crime, horror or action.

ACTIVITIES

1 A large media company approaches a Pacific Island nation with the intention of setting up a television station. The company believes it will make a profit selling the television sets. The company also has access to cheap American television programs which they could screen. Advertising companies also want to sell their products in the Pacific and a foreign government wants to screen its particular version of world news to the Pacific nation.

Divide into two groups.

Group 1 represents the large company which wishes to persuade the local village elders about the benefits of television.

Group 2 represents the village elders and chiefs who are sceptical about the effects of television on their culture, particularly on the young. They do not want television screened in their community.

Both sides need to prepare arguments which give their different points of view.

2 Many studies have been done about the effects of television violence. Investigate some of the findings of these studies and report on whether or not you think television violence affects the viewer.

3 Using the poem below as a starting point, write down in what ways Pacific Islanders would have to adjust to life in large cities.

USA Encounter

Cars . . . Noise . . . Sirens
People never stop to chat
Or even say 'hello'
Where are they all hurrying?
This thing says 'Expire'
Wonder what it means.
'Great Sales' a sign says
And above it spells 'Woolworths'
I walk in and 'Clearance' is everywhere
I buy some things I cannot remember
Except that a lady with a painted face
Gives me some blue stamps
'I've no letters to post' I say
But she ignores me
And gives me my change.

There are lots of people here
But no one sees me
Hey, people, I am lost
I am here
We are all here
And we aren't.

Konai Thaman

4 List the advantages and disadvantages of living in a city and living in the Pacific Islands. Where would you prefer to live and why?

Identity

Almost half a century of disruption and population movements in the Pacific have upset the ancient distribution of clans and territories. In some islands, almost half the population has lived for several generations on land where, if old customs still applied, they would have no right to be. Cooperation and sharing has been replaced by ownership and foreign laws. Increasingly, instead of living in communities, people now live in nuclear families and go out to paid work. Sons and daughters leave home to work or study in big cities and then cannot always adjust when they return. Many areas in the interior of islands are empty as the young flock to the cities for employment.

ACTIVITIES

1 What sort of values does American television present, and how would these clash with traditional Pacific Island culture and values?

2 Why can't the Samoans control television content in their own country?

3 Make a comprehensive list of the ways in which one culture can affect another. Explain how an island culture can protect and maintain its own values and customs and yet still work in a cash economy and take advantage of industrialisation.

Conflicting reports

Article 1

> I can provide money when it is needed, and when I agree with the way it is being used, and my family can still live well in the island. At the same time I can live well here. If they need $[NZ]200, I can send it to them, but if I was there growing taro, what could I give them? I am a foreman in a shoe factory. I have passed my exams and have a good job because not many people can do what I can do. But if I went back [to Western Samoa] I couldn't get a job like this, because they buy all their shoes from overseas and there is no shoe factory. I would probably have to work at the plantation, and that's alright, but not as much use for me or the family as working where I am.
>
> *Western Samoan living in New Zealand*

Article 2

I don't know what I would have done without the [widow's] benefit. If I had been in Samoa when my husband had died, I really don't know what would have happened. I suppose at my age I would have had to remarry, otherwise I would have to depend on my children, and we only had two, so it would have been too difficult. In that way, it's been good for me here . . .

Retired Samoan woman living in Australia

Article 3

We were always taught at technical courses about the importance of co-operation. Our tutors used to set us problems, which we had to solve as a group. Everyone was equal in that setting and we shared all the information . . . We had 'buzz sessions' and 'brainstorming', and everyone was supposed to pitch in and share information and ideas . . . But in Samoa, at least where I worked, there was nothing like that . . . You just had to do what the older people said . . . you felt that they felt you ought to listen to them and do what they wanted . . .

Student who studied and worked in New Zealand

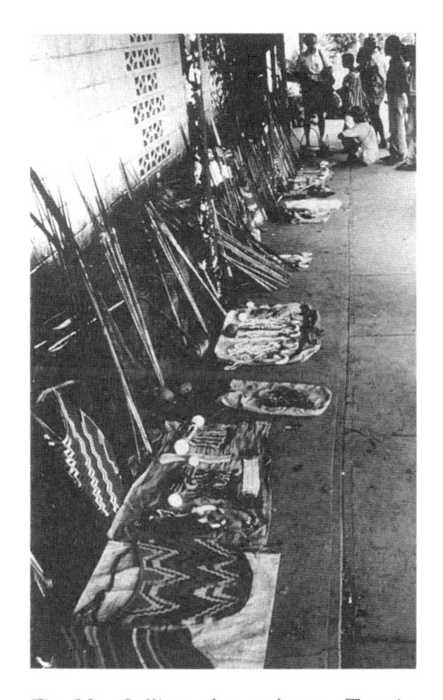

Fig. 39 Selling the culture. Tourist shops sell locally crafted items for the foreign market. Often the real profit is made by the purchasers of this art when they resell it in western countries. How does this help or hinder Pacific Island art and craft?

ACTIVITIES

1 Discuss what the above articles and picture suggest about the extent of the change which has taken place within the traditional family.

2 Explain how the cash economy with its public service, social welfare benefits and employment potential, compares with earlier tradition as a form of security and well-being for the men, women and children in the Pacific.

3 How do you measure 'well-being' for an individual and a culture? For example, is it measured by how much money people have, what political system they have, their happiness, or their religion? What does 'well-being' mean to you?

4 Write an essay responding to this statement. If it wasn't for Western technology, the Pacific Islands would never have developed.

RESEARCH PROJECT

This can be done in groups or pairs. There have been many cases in history when one culture takes over or destroys another. The Spanish invasion and colonisation of South America is just one example. Find another example in history when a similar situation has occurred. Present your findings in a report to the class.

Resources

Billy, A., Lulei, H. & Sipolo, J. (eds) *Mi Mere: Poetry and Prose by Solomon Islands Women Writers*, University of the South Pacific, Solomon Islands Centre, Honiara, 1983.

Chapman, M. & Morrison, P. *Mobility and Identity in the Island Pacific*, a special issue of *Pacific Viewpoint*, Dept of Geography and Victoria University Press, Victoria University, Wellington, NZ in association with East West Centre and the Institute of Pacific Studies, University of the South Pacific, vol. 26, no. 1, 1985.

Hezel, F. 'The dilemmas of development: the effects of modernization on three areas of Island life' and Thomas, P. 'TV: what do we want to watch? Television and video in the Pacific', papers from the 17th Waigoni Seminar, in Stratigos, S. & Hughes, P. (eds) *The Ethics of Development: The Pacific in the 21st Century*, University of Papua New Guinea Press, Port Moresby, 1987, vol. 1, p. 60; vol. 6, p. 23 respectively.

Nesbitt, J. *Development in the Pacific: What Women Say*, Australian Council for Overseas Aid, Development Dossier no. 18, 1986.

South Pacific Social Sciences Association, *Pacific Identity*, a special issue of *Pacific Perspective* (vol. 12, no. 2) Box 5083, Raiwaqa, Fiji, 1984.

THE FIJI COUP

4

Focus question

What was the cause of the Fiji coup in 1987, who has gained from it, and how has it affected Fiji?

▲▲▲ Related questions ▲▲▲

1 What is a coup?

2 What is the Chiefly system in Fiji and how does it work?

3 Who were the main leaders and political forces in Fiji?

4 Was the coup caused by racial differences, economic or strategic factors?

5 How has Fiji been affected by the coup?

In Memoriam

May 14th 1987 will always
be remembered with sorrow and despair
The shocking and
tragic news was very hard to bear,
The tears in our eyes we
can wipe away,
But the ache in our hearts
will always stay, the memories we have are
like threads of gold,
They will never tarnish or grow old,
Gone is the freedom we
loved so dear,
Silent is the voice of
conscience we long to
hear.
Our parting came so
suddenly
We are all still wondering
why?
But the hardest part of all
We were never given a choice.
Sadly missed by the silenced
majority voice.

Fiji Sun, 8 August 1987

Fig. 40 What was Colonel Rabuka's role in the Fiji coup?

Asked what gave him the inspiration to overthrow Dr Bavadra's new Fiji Labour Party National Coalition Government, Colonel Rabuka said 'I strongly believe the inspiration came from God'. *Fiji Times*, 6 July 1987

14 May 1987

It was a warm Fijian day as the newly elected parliamentarians, in their traditional costume, ascended the steps into Parliament House. Some were discussing the recent demonstrations in Suva and others stood under the hot sun preparing for the day's debate. Fiji had been independent from the British for seventeen years and it was a model of democracy in the South Pacific. How many of the parliamentarians knew what was going to happen that day? Did they have any reason to be suspicious?

In the air-conditioned parliament they sat in rows listening to the debates as Dr Timoci Bavadra's new Fiji Labour/National Party Coalition Government introduced its reforms.

At first there was shouting and movement. Suddenly, to the horror of the new parliamentarians, ten masked men with machine guns stormed into the chamber, ordering everyone to be silent. Nobody moved. The masked gunmen were wearing military fatigues.

'Sit down, everybody, sit down. This is a takeover. Ladies and gentlemen, this is a military takeover.'

The leader then announced that a military coup was removing the government and everyone was to leave. Surrounding the Parliament were more soldiers in balaclavas nervously wielding machine guns. All the parliamentarians from the new coalition government were arrested and taken away in trucks to military barracks near Suva, the capital of Fiji.

The man behind the mask was Colonel Sitiveni Rabuka who proclaimed himself head of the country and declared a state of emergency. The new Bavadra government had ended, so too had democracy in Fiji.

Minutes later, the news flashed across the world: Fiji had been taken over by a military coup.

The coup

Read this newspaper article and answer the following questions.

Governor pleads for an end to Fiji coup

By a special correspondent,
Suva, Friday

The Governor-General of Fiji, Ratu Sir Penaia Ganilau, last night announced he had assumed executive power and proclaimed "a state of public emergency" after an army colonel overthrew the Government of Fiji yesterday.

But it appeared that the new regime of Lieutenant-Colonel Sitiveni Rabuka had moved to stifle the Governor-General's proclamation. Radio Fiji was prevented from broadcasting it and the regime placed a guard on Government House and disconnected the telephone.

Early yesterday, Colonel Rabuka led a team of soldiers into Parliament in Suva and rounded up the Prime Minister, Dr Timoci Bavadra, and 27 members of the Government.

Late last night Dr Bavadra and his ministers were taken from Suva's Queen Elizabeth barracks to their own homes which were kept under guard.

In a surprising development early today the former Fiji Prime Minister, Ratu Sir Kamisese Mara, was named Foreign Affairs Minister of an interim council of ministers, in a radio announcement by Colonel Rabuka.

Fifteen ministries were allotted, six of them to members of the Alliance Party ministry defeated in elections last month by the National Federation Party-Labour Party coalition.

Colonel Rabuka's announcement said those nominated to the council had been summoned, accepted and would meet at 11 am today.

In his proclamation last night, Sir Penaia said he was taking immediate steps to "restore the lawful situation". He called on all members of the army, police and public service "to return to their lawful allegiance". The message was broadcast on a commercial radio station.

The Prime Minister, Mr Hawke, said last night that his "most optimistic hope" was that the Governor-General's proclamation might change the course of events.

Colonel Rabuka, the third ranking officer in the Royal Fiji Military Forces, told a news conference that he had acted to head off militant Fijians who planned to disrupt the Government and also to stop the Government calling out the troops against them.

Telex and telephone communications between Fiji and overseas countries were cut or restricted and the national station, Radio Fiji, was ordered to broadcast no information other than that released by Colonel Rabuka.

In CANBERRA, the commander in chief of the Fijian armed forces, Brigadier Ratu Epeli Nailatikau, left Parliament House last night after a 40-minute meeting with Mr Hawke, claiming he was still in charge of the armed forces.

Both Mr Hawke and the brigadier discounted the possibility of military action by Australia, although Mr Hawke did say he was "open" on the question of whether two Royal Australian Navy ships already in Fiji should prolong their stay.

Brigadier Nailatikau said there were "no circumstances at all" in which he would seek Australian intervention.

He said Mr Hawke had made an offer of help but would not comment further: "What I have to do is wait and see what the situation is like in Fiji,'' he said.

Last night Fiji was in shock and the Indian community, roughly half the population, was cowed and nervous.

Long queues formed at the banks throughout yesterday, as people withdrew their money, and travel agents reported a dramatic jump in requests for tickets and travel arrangements.

The coup was a climax to discontent among some Fijian people over the Indian majority in the new Government.

Street marches and protest meetings have been held in several parts of the country since the election of 4 to 11 April. The Governor-General and the Prime Minister appealed for calm after a democratic election.

No unrest was reported yesterday outside the capital, although unconfirmed reports early in the evening said a roadblock had been thrown up at the village of Veseisei in the province of Vuda.

The *Age*

---

1 From the information provided what do you think a 'coup' is?

2 Does the article give any reasons for the coup?

3 Can you suggest other reasons? Who would gain from the coup?

4 Who are the main people behind the coup and why did they carry it out?

5 What happens to the rights of individuals during and after a coup when a state of emergency is declared?

ACTIVITY

Can you list any other countries which have experienced a coup? What reasons were given by the coup leaders and what were the results of the coup?

Background to Fiji

Fiji is well known for its beauty, climate and friendly culture. It is a well known tourist destination for French, Australian, German and American visitors. Its beautiful beaches and tropical forests are sought-after refuges for people looking for quiet, pollution-free holidays.

Fiji consists of over 320 islands of which 105 are inhabited. The main islands are Viti Levu (the largest island with the capital Suva), Vanua Levu, Taveuni and Lau, all of which are spread over some 160 000 square kilometres of ocean (see Fig. 42). The total land area of Fiji is 18 000 square kilometres. Fiji has a fast-growing population. In 1987 it was estimated to be 715 000.

Fijian ethnic culture is diverse. In 1987 there were two main groups within the population, the Indians and the indigenous Fijians. Indians were mainly descendants of indentured labourers brought into Fiji by the British to work in the sugar plantations in the 19th century. A third, minor, group is European.

Fig. 41 Fijian beaches are a major tourist attraction. How would tourism help the island?

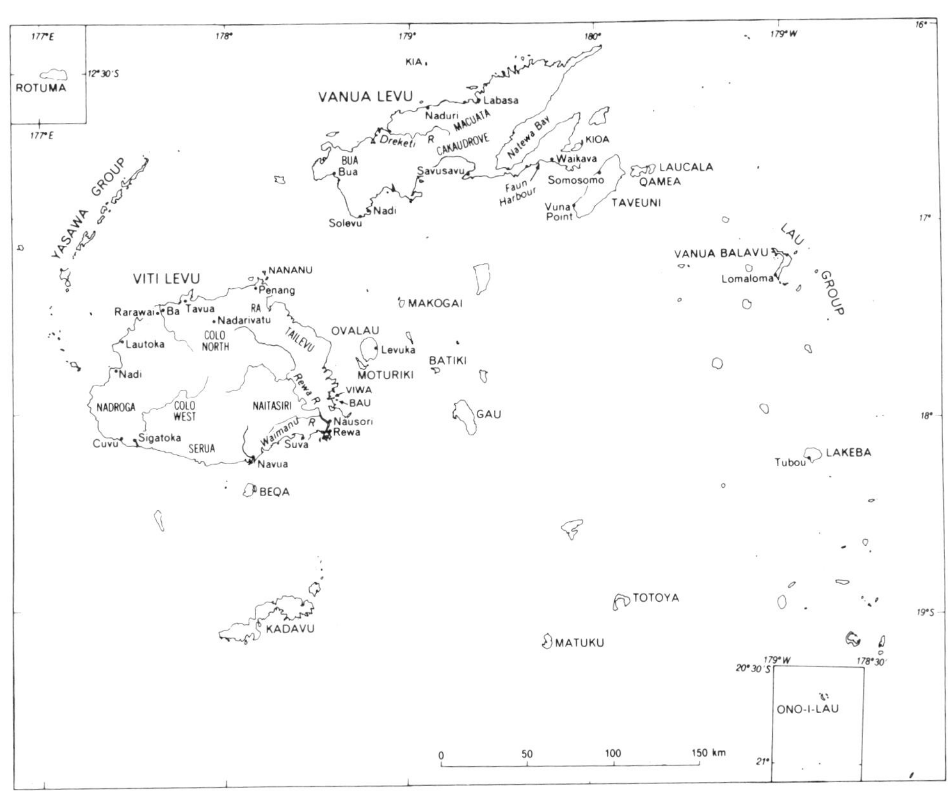

Fig. 42 Map of Fiji.

Ethnic culture

Indians	350 000 or 50% of the population
Indigenous Fijians	336 000 or 47%

The remaining 29 000 are either European, or part European and Chinese.

Religious belief

Christian	51%	Hindu	40%	Muslim	8%

Language

The official language is English but most people also speak either a Fijian dialect or Hindi, an Indian language.

Fig. 43 Ratu Sir Penaia Ganilau. Who are the Ratus?

Ratus or Chiefs

In Fijian society the Chief holds a highly esteemed social position. People believed that the power of the gods was embodied in him.

ACTIVITY

Divide into groups and research one of the following aspects of Fijian society. Each group can report back to the class with their findings.

- ▲ education
- ▲ sport
- ▲ political system
- ▲ traditional dress
- ▲ role of the Chiefs or Ratus
- ▲ art, literature and religion
- ▲ role of men, women and children

History of Fiji

The first European to visit Fiji was Abel Tasman in 1643. Captain Cook visited in 1774. It was not long after that traders came to Fiji for sandalwood and whalers from Australia, New Zealand and America passed through.

Next came the Christian missionaries seeking new converts. In 1874, under the Fijian Chief Cakobau, Fiji ceded to Britain because the Fijian Chief was concerned that Germany would annex the island. Soon after, under colonial rule, the British established sugar plantations between 1879 and 1916. These plantations were established to bring in some income for the British colony to make it economically independent from Britain and to provide it with cheap, raw materials.

In order to run the sugar plantations, the British brought Indian workers over to Fiji. The indigenous Fijians did not want to work on the plantations, instead, they preferred their basic subsistence farming and had little interest in, or need for, a cash economy.

In 1931 Indian immigration was stopped but as early as 1888 the Ratus or Chiefs had expressed their opinion that the Indians should be returned after a five year period.

> Though we do not wish to be inhospitable, yet, we cannot help observing that their number is increasing and that they are becoming a source of annoyance to us by their customs which are entirely different from our own and distasteful to us.

On the one hand the Ratus did not mind the Indians coming in and earning money for Fiji, but on the other they wanted to get rid of them. The Fijians relied on the Fijian Indians to maintain the economy and raise government revenue through taxes while the Indians rented Fijian land; both needed each other.

Fiji was ruled by its traditional system of hereditary Chiefs or Ratus. The highest Chiefs come together in The Great Council of Chiefs and they are the respected elders in Fijian society. The Ratus are powerful men in Fijian society and they have tried to stop change which has affected the traditional values of their culture. Even today, many indigenous Fijians still live subsistence lives on the land. However, social change, employment, schooling and large towns have changed some of these social customs including the distribution of political power. Prior to independence, when the new constitution was being discussed, the Great Chiefs stated:

> Democracy . . . meant rule by ignorance and prejudice . . . forces as nefarious and ruinous, whether they be in alliance with Europeans, Indians or Fijians . . . we choose, with full support of native conservative and liberal opinion, the system of nomination believing that along this road, and along it alone, the principle of trusteeship for the Fijian race can be preserved and the paramountcy of native interest secured.

The Fijian Chiefs were not just interested in 'protecting' their culture, but also in maintaining their own power, especially from the wealthy Indian merchants and traders who had money but no land. The Indo–Fijians wanted to protect themselves from the Ratus by having one person, one vote so the Ratus had no special status or position over them. On the whole, despite the Ratus' concerns about the Indians, the ordinary Fijians and Indians worked side by side for the common good of Fiji.

The Ratus worked with the British during the colonial years because it helped them maintain power and status. It also benefited the British in terms of controlling the Fijian population if the Ratus were on their side and did what they asked them because this limited the British involvement directly with the ordinary Fijians. When the British left, the Ratus were not going to be deprived of their position after Fiji's independence. Instead the Ratus decided not to rely on British protection but claimed that because they were 'sons of the soil . . . this Colony must be handed over into the hands of the Fijians'.

In 1965 a major Conference was held in London to write a new Fijian constitution and to prepare Fiji for independence from Britain. In 1966 the British introduced a new constitution which provided for a ministerial form of government. The British were not so concerned about the role of the Ratus so long as both sides felt satisfied and everyone had a vote.

ACTIVITY

Discuss in class what is meant by a ministerial form of government. Give examples of other countries which have a similar system.

Independence, 1970

After independence in 1970, the first general election was won by the Alliance Party which largely represented the indigenous Fijians. They campaigned on the need to protect 'native interests' in the face of what they saw as a threat from a growing Indian population. They also won many wealthy Indian voters who had made money and were prepared to work with the government which would protect their interests too. However, the Alliance Party also claimed to be multi-racial, representing all the interests in Fiji.

On the other hand, the Fijian citizens of Indian origin were mostly represented by the National Federation Party which protested against what they felt was discrimination against them in the constitution. In September, 1967, the NFP called for another conference. They resigned in protest when a review was not held because they felt the indigenous Fijians were entrenched in the electoral system. Generally, however, there were good relations between the Fijians and Indo–Fijians. Racial tension, when it did occur, was usually the result of a minority. Racial tension did emerge in some by-elections when the Indians perceived injustice and, because of this hostility, both the leaders of the Alliance Party and the National Federation Party met and a further constitutional conference was held in London.

Major issues arising from the 1965 Conference on Independence

1 The Ratus wanted to keep the ownership of the land. In fact, they owned 83 per cent and the existing law prohibited the sale of land by indigenous people. Land was traditionally owned by family groups. It was either reserved or unreserved land. Unreserved land could be leased to non-indigenous Fijians for up to a period of thirty years. In effect this law denied over half the population ownership of the land. They also did not want what they saw as non-indigenous Fijians replacing their own culture.

2 The Indo–Fijians make up 95 per cent of the sugar-cane workers, one of Fiji's highest income earners representing three-fifths of her export earnings. Many of the Indians live on small farms rented to them by the Chiefs. Other Indians run business in Suva. In fact, the Indian community ran the cash economy in Fiji and it was the Indians who made Fiji wealthy through the sugar plantations and the taxes which went to the government.

3 The Indo–Fijians, who were very active in the movement for independence from Britain, wanted their interests protected from the Ratus through a Westminster-style government. They wanted one person, one vote, irrespective of race. They did not want the Chiefs to have any special control in the Parliament.

In the 1970 Constitution, the Lower House of Parliament was distributed according to race. Twenty-two seats were reserved for Fijians, twenty-two for Indians and eight for other communities (mainly European and Chinese).

ACTIVITIES

1 Working in pairs and using the information above, draw a time-line of events which have taken place in Fiji since 1643.

2 Divide into three groups. Each group represents a delegation to the 1965 Conference on the Fiji Constitution. Each group must prepare views on the new Constitution after independence is declared.

Group 1 represents the Ratus or Chiefs. Examine the Ratus' statements and prepare their case. What are their concerns? Examine the quote:

> Democracy . . . meant rule by ignorance and prejudice . . . forces as nefarious and ruinous, whether they be in alliance with Europeans, Indians or Fijians . . . we choose, with full support of native conservative and liberal opinion, the system of nomination believing that along this road, and along it alone, the principle of trusteeship for the Fijian race can be preserved and the paramountcy of native interest secured.

Also refer to the major issues listed above.

Group 2 represents the Indo–Fijians. Refer to major issues 2 and 3. What are their concerns? Why do you think they want a democratic system without the Chiefs or Ratus? Present a case and arguments supporting the type of Constitution they would prefer.

Group 3 represents the British. They want to make sure that Fiji is democratic and economically secure. They also want it to remain a friendly ally in the Pacific. They want to get out of Fiji but not at any price. They recognise the racial situation and they want to consider each group's case.

Each group should present their views on the question: How will democracy be achieved in Fiji after independence?

3 Write answers to these questions.

a Why did Chief Cakobau want to cede Fiji to the British?
b Who are the Ratus and what is their role in Fijian society?
c Why did the British bring the Indians to Fiji?
d How did the Ratus view the Indian labourers?
e Why was a Westminster system, one person, one vote, unacceptable to the Ratus?
f Why did the Indo–Fijian population want one person, one vote?
g Who owned most of the land and why?
h What two major political parties emerged and who did they represent?
i Who was earning the most revenue for the government and how?

4 Discuss in class what you think are the early underlying causes of tension between the Fijians and Indo–Fijians.

5 The British brought Indians over to work on the sugar plantations in Fiji. Research other examples in history of colonial powers bringing cheap labour (including slaves) to work on their investments. What were the later consequences of these actions?

6 Read the following conflicting views on colonialism. The quotes come from *Teaching Development Issues* (see 'Resources' below).

The African is my brother, but he is my junior brother.
(Albert Schweitzer, who ran a mission hospital in Central Africa.)

Law and order is perhaps the most important advantage that we British gave to our colonies. People could go about their daily lives without fear of attack by others. Also our nation's record in abolishing slavery is a commendable fact. We took the ideas of liberty, equality, justice and democracy to the colonies and with these came advantages of civilisation closely followed by benefits of technology.

What were these advantages? First, ease of travel, secondly education, thirdly public health. Apart from the fight against disease our experts helped to provide sanitation and pure water supplies. Also there were improvements in agriculture. The products . . . could be sold at a profit.
(A British Colonial Administrator)

We have been oppressed a great deal, we have been exploited a great deal and we have been disregarded a great deal.
(Julius Nyerere, President of Tanzania)

Even when our children got education they found all the top jobs were kept for whites.
(An Indian)

The wages paid in mines were very low and we got terrible diseases. On the plantations we sometimes had to work for nothing; it was almost like slavery.
(An African)

With reference to the above statements, write an essay discussing the following: It was the unequal economic relationship, originating in the colonial period, that has created division and poverty in the Third World.

Events leading up to the coup

Read the newspaper article on the opposite page, then read the fifteen statements below.

These statements present some of the main issues leading up to the 1987 election. The two major parties contesting the election were the Alliance Party and the Fiji Labour Party/National Party Coalition. The Alliance Party had been in power for seventeen years since gaining independence from Britain.

Statement 1

The Alliance Party had been in power for seventeen years and the economy was on the decline. The Alliance leader, Ratu Kamisese Mara, had put many of his friends in positions of power (patronage) and there were allegations of corruption.

How the military takeover unfolded

THIS is a chronology of events leading up to and following yesterday's coup (all times, Suva time):

April 12: Coalition led by Dr Timoci Bavadra defeats Ratu Sir Kamisese Mara's Alliance Party in an election in which antipathy between descendants of Indian migrant sugar workers and indigenous Fijian islanders featured prominently.

April 14: Dr Bavadra announces a cabinet comprising mainly Indian Fijians.

April 21: Traditional chiefs meeting on Viti Levu island call for marches in major centres to demand guarantees of special status for indigenous Fijians.

April 23: Protest marches are held, including one by 5,500 people in Suva, who petition the Governor-General for constitutional changes to ensure Fijian leadership.

April 24: Dr Bavadra makes radio broadcast calling for people not to be misled by a few "bent on destroying democracy".

April 26: Mr Apisai Tora, formerly Communications Minister under Ratu Sir Kamisese Mara, announces a campaign of civil disobedience.

April 27: Alliance Party's leading Indian member quits because, he says, Fijian party supporters are destroying multi-racial character of what is now the Opposition party.

May 4: The Attorney-General's offices and four other buildings are petrol-bombed in Lautoka, Fiji's second city.

May 6: Permission denied for rally of government opponents when Parliament reopens on May 8.

May 10: Fijians of all parties are invited to join a Fiji United Front to give the outnumbered indigenous Fijians a united voice on national issues. A government spokesman denounces the front as "mischievous".

May 11: Mr Tora is charged with sedition and inciting racial antagonism at the traditional chiefs' meeting on April 21.

May 14, 10 am: Lieutenant-Colonel Sitiveni Rabuka and 10 men march into the House of Representatives Chamber brandishing pistols.

Government members are marched outside where they are loaded into army trucks and taken to an unknown destination.

• The Information Ministry issues a statement saying the army has taken over the Government.

It says Colonel Rabuka has gone to Government House to see the Governor-General, Ratu Sir Penaia Ganilau, to seek recognition for the Government.

The colonel says he will meet the Diplomatic Corps at 2 pm before holding a news conference.

• Ratu Sir Kamisese Mara, who has been chairing a conference at Sigatoka, 125 kilometres west of Suva, is reported to be on his way back to Suva by road.

11 am: Communications between Australia and Fiji are cut, says a Foreign Affairs official in Canberra.

• New Zealand's Prime Minister, Mr Lange, meets senior Foreign Affairs officials to discuss the coup.

Noon: Colonel Rabuka says he wants to assure all next-of-kin of the safety of the 28 government members.

• Australia's acting High Commissioner in Suva, Mr Peter Stanford, says there are no indications that there will be violence, but tells Australians in Fiji calling for advice to "be careful".

1 pm: Federal Government officials estimate that 2,200 Australian tourists are in Fiji, but say there is no cause for relatives or friends to be alarmed.

• Telephone and telex links with Fiji restored.

2 pm: Chiefs of mission from Suva's embassies, high commissions and consulates arrive at the main government building in Suva and prepare to meet Colonel Rabuka.

• The New Zealand armed forces are expected to move to a readiness footing after an emergency Cabinet meeting, says a news report.

• A spokesman for the acting Minister for Foreign Affairs, Senator Evans, says that as far as he is aware no request has been made for Australian involvement in the situation from the Government of Dr Timoci Bavadra.

• Mr Hawke issues strict orders to Australian High Commission staff in Fiji not to attend any meeting or press conference held by Colonel Rabuka.

• In Wellington, Mr Lange deplores the coup and vows not to co-operate with military officers reportedly about to declare a provisional Government.

• Diplomats are briefed by Colonel Rabuka.

3 pm: Colonel Rabuka tells the news conference that he organised the coup to pre-empt the Government calling out the army to act against Fijians plotting against the Government.

He will neither confirm nor deny rumours of Soviet and Libyan influences leading to the coup.

4 pm: Mr Hawke says the commander of the Royal Fiji Military Force, Brigadier-General Ratu Epeli Nailatikau, is in Australia for a weekend ceremony in Perth involving the handover of a patrol boat. He does not indicate the General's reaction to the coup or when the general will be returning to Fiji.

5 pm: News reports suggest Ratu Sir Kamisese Mara is back in Suva.

• Mr Lange says Brigadier Ratu Epeli Nailatikau is on his way back to Suva on a RAAF aircraft but the Defence Department denies that the RAAF is to fly the brigadier to Fiji.

8 pm: The Governor-General announces he has assumed executive power under the Constitution and says he has declared "a state of public emergency".

Sydney Morning Herald

Fig. 44 Indo-Fijian shops in Suva, the capital of Fiji. Describe their appearance.

Statement 2

At the beginning of 1985, Fiji experienced five cyclones. Food shortages followed and prices rose rapidly. Some insurance companies raised their rates by 1000 times. For the poor, the cyclones made the gap between the rich and the poor wider.

Fig. 45 Cyclone damage. Cyclones cause havoc to the economy of a Pacific island. What sorts of aid would be needed?

Statement 3

By 1986 newspapers were reporting an alarming growth in destitution . . . A Suva City Council survey reported that one in every eight Suva residents lived in twenty-six squatter colonies and were subject to poor sewerage and water facilities, and unhealthy crowded living conditions. [Two-thirds of all Fijian households were at risk of poverty].

Statement 4

In 1986, the Minister for Home Affairs, Akariva Nabati, called the increase in crime 'enormous'. Between 1985 and 1986, rape offences doubled and burglaries and break-ins rose by 37 per cent.

Statement 5

In 1985, Fiji exported $1 million worth of clothing. However, wages were low and workers were earning an average of seventy-four cents an hour.

Statement 6

In 1985, farmers were warned that sugar prices would fall to $17.50 per tonne, barely enough to cover their production costs. As the world price of sugar fell so did production. The Fiji Sugar Corporation made a loss of $6.6 million in 1985–86. At the same time, due to the cyclones, the number of tourists visiting Fiji declined.

Fig. 46 Slums in Fiji. Why do slums occur in these beautiful Pacific islands which are the centre of major tourism?

Statement 7

The Ratus, who controlled the Native Lands Trust Board and rented land to Indo–Fijian farmers were making huge profits. This caused resentment both from ordinary Fijians who were getting only a small share of rent money and Indo–Fijians.

Statement 8

Domestic workers were the most exploited of the Fiji work force. Women also undertook 80 per cent of the manual agricultural labour and receive little training and assistance.

Statement 9

Under the Alliance, the elite have feathered their own nests while conditions for the rest, particularly the poor and disadvantaged, have got steadily worse. Inequalities have become part and parcel of Alliance rule. Poverty is a disease — the Alliance is the carrier. (*Fiji Sun*, 2 April 1987)

Statement 10

In 1983, without any warning or discussion, the Alliance Party lifted a ban on US nuclear-powered and armed warships visiting Fiji. Fiji had, in the past, banned such visits. This caused resentment from members of both races who wanted to remain non-aligned and nuclear-free.

Fig. 47 US warships docked at Suva, Fiji.

Statement 11

The new Fiji Labour Party, under Bavadra, declared that it would restore the anti-nuclear ban and express its displeasure at US actions in the Pacific, in particular, its refusal to sign the Treaty of Rarotonga, declaring the Pacific a Nuclear-Free Zone.

Statement 12

Allegations of corruption and mismanagement dogged the Alliance Party during its election campaign. Tupeni Baba claimed that since 1982 government vehicles had been involved in 1445 accidents. In 1985 the Inland Revenue Department failed to collect some $8.8 million in taxes. Baba alleges that the National Bank of Fiji wrote off $4 million owed by the Stinson Pearce Group. Lautoka lawyer Bhupendra Patel claimed evidence in March that garment manufacturers paid $52 000 to the Alliance Party to prevent the enforcement of minimum wages.

Statement 13

Concerned that young Fijians would vote for the new Fiji Labour Party, the Alliance Party turned to racist fear tactics. They argued that, without the Alliance Government, land rights would be in jeopardy and without land Fijians would be nobody.

Statement 14

On 21 March Bavadra alleged that the Alliance Party's abuse of Chiefly power (Ratus) demonstrated unequal sharing of funding for the different regions. The Alliance Prime Minister's province of Lau, with a population of 14 000 people, received $1.3 million dollars while the province of Ba received only $400 000 for 59 000 Fijians.

Statement 15

The Ratus supported the Alliance Party because they were able to put many of their relatives and friends into positions of power who were then able to distribute wealth for their own benefit.

ACTIVITIES

1. From the above statements compile a newspaper article identifying why you think the Fiji Labour Party won the election.

2. Divide the class into groups of five. Each group should represent either the Labour Coalition or the Alliance Party. Each group should examine the fifteen statements and prepare a report which argues why Fijians should vote for the particular party and refutes criticisms made about their party.

Your report should include political posters which present your party in the best possible way. When the report and posters are finished one group member can address the class.

After all the speeches have been made, answer the following questions.

a What do you think were the major issues which led up to the election of the new Labour Government?

b Who would have gained from a Fiji Labour victory and why?

c Who would have gained from an Alliance victory and why?

d Do you think 'race' played a major role in the election result? Give reasons for your answer.

e What had happened to the Fijian economy prior to the election?

f How would a Fiji Labour victory affect the Ratus?

g Why do you think young, urban indigenous Fijians were voting for the new Labour Party?

h Which party would the United States have supported and why?

3 Read these articles and then answer the following questions.

Bavadra claim: 'CIA funded coup'

The deposed Prime Minister, Dr Timoci Bavadra, claimed in Washington yesterday that a Suva-based American diplomat had given $188,000 ($US200,000) to an "Opposition activist" involved in the revolt against Dr Bavadra's government.

Dr Bavadra identified the man as the Director of US Agency for International Development with the American Embassy in Suva, Mr William Paupe, and said that he was linked to the Central Intelligence Agency (CIA).

But the American Embassy in Suva strongly denied the allegations or any links with the military coup in Fiji and said Dr Bavadra's allegations were "ludicrous".

Dr Bavadra repeated his call for the United States Congress to probe possible American involvement in the military coup of May 14 which toppled his government.

Reuters reported from Washington DC, at a news conference Dr Bavadra suggested elements of a private US network associated with the Iran-Contra affair may have been involved.

An aide, Dr James Anthony, described one US embassy employee in Suva as a "barefoot Ollie North", a reference to the fired White House aide at the centre of the scandal over covert arms sales to Iran and the diversion of profits to the Nicaraguan Contra rebels.

Dr Anthony and Dr Bavadra both identified the employee as Mr William Paupe, director of the Suva office of the US Agency for International Development (AID).

Dr Bavadra said he had information Mr Paupe had paid $US200,000 to an opposition activist to stir up a revolt.

"Democracy had been raped," said Dr Bavadra, 52, a medical doctor who took office on April 13 after elections ended a 17-year hold on power by the Alliance Party. He was ousted in a coup on May 14.

Dr Bavadra said he wanted the Congressional probe to determine whether the coup was an official US intelligence operation, in private hands "or was an operation that was a combination of . . . both these themes".

Fiji Times

Rabuka's bully boys decide what's free

SINCE Colonel Rabuka's second coup, there has been a spate of reports of psychological and physical harassment of people detained by the military and police. The *Herald* has copies of several signed and witnessed reports by former detainees, which shed light on the growing abuse of human rights in Fiji since the military resumed control on September 25.

The Fiji Red Cross, working until this week without assistance from its international headquarters in Geneva, has been able to confirm 57 detentions on political grounds. Others in Fiji claim the figure may be twice as high, if the continued cases of overnight detention are included.

The main targets of Colonel Rabuka's Government — which in Decree No 9, dated October 13, changed its name from the Fiji Interim Military Government to Fiji Military Government — appear to be members or relatives of the deposed Coalition Government, people involved in the "Back to early May movement" which opposed the first coup, and almost anyone else suspected of agitating against the regime.

In stark contrast to Rabuka's "friendly coup" in May, his second takeover was executed with much greater precision and forward planning. While Colonel Rabuka has promised elections in a year's time and still speaks of a return to normalcy, a sharper awareness of how to control political activity is evident in his Government's current actions and policies. Actions taken on and since September 25 have effectively silenced opposition to the republican regime.

The closure of the presses, censorship of the radio, suspension of the Supreme Court, the silencing of the Governor-General, the closing of trade unions, the ban on political meetings, and the dusk-to-dawn curfew, have effectively given Colonel Rabuka and his colleagues complete political, as well as logistical, control over the country.

The most effective technique is the arrest and detention of any person suspected of actively opposing the regime. But as in any police state, the neutralisation of such people often means that others not even guilty of agitating for a return to democracy are being detained on the basis of rumour or circumstantial evidence.

Sydney Morning Herald

Indian protest cripples Fiji

Suva, Thursday — APP

Business life in cities and towns across Fiji stopped or was severely disrupted today as the country's 350,000 Indians staged a 24-hour shutdown in protest against the firebombing of three temples and a mosque last weekend.

Indian community leaders hailed the peaceful stoppage as the most successful act of solidarity by their people since similar strikes after two military coups in 1987 that ousted the Indian-dominated coalition Government.

Tonight, the leaders of the country's six main Hindu organisations also cancelled public celebrations scheduled in 11 days to mark their religion's festival of light, Diwali, roughly the Hindu equivalent of Christmas.

While the effects of the stoppage were mixed in the capital Suva, the Indian-dominated western centres of Ba, Sigatoka and Nadi plus the northern town of Labasa came almost to a standstill.

The full force of the stoppage was felt in Fiji's second city, Lautoka, where the arson attacks were allegedly committed by a gang of hymn-singing indigenous Fijian Methodists early on Sunday.

The group of 18 have been arrested and if convicted of arson could be jailed for life.

Normally bustling streets were empty as thousands stayed at home. Shops, except for non-Indian-owned supermarkets, remained shut. Banks and other business houses also were forced to close as Indian staff stayed away from work.

Government offices were affected and the cutting of cane for Fiji's vital sugar harvest stopped.

An estimated 80 per cent of Indian-run schools were closed as part of an escalating weeklong parallel protest by students, parents and teachers.

About 700 Indian students from the Suva-based University of the South Pacific also boycotted classes.

The *Age*

Rabuka bans all political, union action

From correspondents in Suva

ALL political activity in Fiji has been banned by the military government, Radio Fiji said yesterday.

A news broadcast by the government-controlled network was the first local publicity on the latest of a series of decrees from Colonel Sitiveni Rabuka's republican leadership.

Radio Fiji reported part of a decree that "individuals will be free to form or belong to a trade union or association to protect his or her interests".

But the report omitted to mention a ban on "industrial action by trade unions, in the form of strikes, bans, go-slow campaigns, protest marches and demonstrations".

The broadcast said: "The suspension applies to all political parties, groups or affiliations in the interest of public order or safety."

The *Australian*

4 Who do you think gained from the coup and why? Who lost because of the coup and why?

- ▲ Chiefs
- ▲ Alliance Party
- ▲ United States
- ▲ Taukei Movement
- ▲ Indo–Fijians
- ▲ Labour Coalition

5 Why do you think most democratic countries around the world condemned the coup?

6 How do coup leaders keep themselves in power?

7 What do you think are the long-term problems of living under military dictatorship?

RESEARCH PROJECT

Go back to the front page article announcing the coup. Does it fully explain the major events leading up to the coup and the reason why it happened? What do newspapers leave out? How well informed are we about world events through reading the newspapers? What other sources should we look at to gain a better understanding of the events in Fiji?

From your understanding of this coup, how vulnerable do you believe countries are to military coups? Investigate and present a report on a coup that has taken place in a country other than Fiji.

Resources

Lal, V. B. *Politics in Fiji*, Allen & Unwin, Melbourne, 1986.

Robertson, R. & Tamanisau, A. *Shattered Coups*, Pluto Press, Australia, 1988.

Standish, B. 'End of "A New Era. Towards Interpretation" ', Background Paper, Department of Foreign Affairs, 1987.

Teaching Development Issues (Section 2 Colonialism), Development Education Project, Manchester Polytechnic, Manchester M20 8RG, UK.

5 New Caledonia: Human Rights and Independence

Focus question

Since the French occupied New Caledonia there has been continued violence between the French settlers and the indigenous Kanaks. What is the nature of this conflict and why do the Kanaks want independence?

▲▲▲ Related questions ▲▲▲

1 Who are the Kanaks?

2 Why are the French in New Caledonia?

3 Since the first French settlements, how have the Kanaks been treated?

4 What are the different ways in which the French and the Kanaks view land rights?

5 In what ways do the French and Kanak cultures differ?

6 What are the future options for New Caledonia?

Interview with Dewe Gorodey

Dewe Gorodey, a member of the Kanak Socialist National Liberation Front (FLNKS), has been imprisoned several times by the French authorities for her outspoken views and political activities. She was interviewed in 1978.

> Since the beginning of French occupation in New Caledonia the Kanak [Kanak means human being] tribes have constantly rebelled. The most important early Kanak struggle took place in 1878 under the leadership of High Chief Atai. The main cause of these struggles was the alienation of land.
>
> [Before the French occupied our land in 1853], the Kanak economy was based on agriculture, working the land . . . land was not considered to be something that could be sold or exchanged. On the contrary, it was regarded as a mother, a wife, a human being and, above all, as the spiritual source of life for the Kanak. Kanaks maintain relations with the land based on respect; a respect equal to that accorded to everything which surrounds them: the human, the natural, the supernatural . . .

When the missionaries came to impose their Christianity on the Kanak people, it was the framework of a system which denies the existence of coloured people . . .

When the French admiral Febvrier Despointes, supported by the colonial army and missionaries, took possession of New Caledonia on September 4 1853, he legalised and made official the pillage of land, the destruction of a culture, and the slow death of the Kanak people.

Fig. 48 FLNKS leaders in New Caledonia. Why was the FLNKS established?

ACTIVITIES

1 Write answers to these questions.

a Who are the Kanaks?

b What is the Kanak Socialist National Liberation Front (FLNKS)? (The initials come from the French: *Front de Liberation Nationale, Kanak et Socialiste.*)

c What has been the role of the French in New Caledonia?

d What do you think is the Kanak attitude towards the land and how would this differ from the French approach?

2 Discuss in class what you think has happened to the Kanaks in New Caledonia since the French colonised the islands in 1853.

Before French colonisation

The basic unit of Kanak life has always been lineage. The lineage is a kin group that is traced through the females in the family back to the oldest surviving woman. Hence a woman and her children (but not her husband), her sisters and

Fig. 49 Members of families living together are called 'kin'. Describe the clothing worn by the kin. Is it traditional? How does it reflect the artistic abilities of these people?

their children, her brothers (but not their wives or children), her aunts and uncles through her mother's side, and her maternal grandmother would make up the lineage group. This lineage group formerly lived together on the lineage estate and ate what was produced from the land belonging to the lineage. The lineage group would be up to two or three households, each with a single nuclear family and perhaps the addition of some other relatives.

The members of these households, especially the younger ones, were subject to the authority of the lineage Chief, the senior man in the lineage. He was empowered to oversee the lineage land, assign work responsibilities to other members of the lineage and supervise the distribution of the food among them. When a woman married, she would generally bring her husband to her own lineage's estate where her children would be raised in their kin group and her husband could discharge his responsibilities to the family. The groups ate together, worked together, and their children were raised together. The single cookhouse in which food was prepared represented the unity of the lineage as a social group.

Individuals and land rights

An individual had the right to use the land of his clan. A clan member's right of cultivation could not be given to a stranger except by the master of the land, who received a customary offering of harvested products. A non-member's right to cultivate could be renewed year after year.

The power over agriculture lay with the master of the land who was one of the most influential of the council elders. He was often head of the longest running established clan and his power derived from the fact that he was assumed to be the direct descendant of the first occupant. He arbitrated land disputes between clans.

A fundamental principle is that the land is always family property. Its usage is linked to the individual's membership of the family group or to acceptance by that group. But all the produce was the property of those who did the work on the land. Even if the land belonged to another clan, the planter retained an individual right to the plants cultivated by him or her.

Land rights came mainly from the right to first occupancy, that is, who was there first. Once established, these rights were sacred and difficult to change. Sometimes clans transferred land which was compensated by gifts or services.

Melanesian Land Rights were derived from first known occupancy. Economic power and political power were quite separate. This delicate and longstanding system of land ownership and village living was destroyed in the second half of the 19th century by French colonisation. On many of the islands the indigenous population was pushed back into the highlands and was confined in reserves, situated in the most hilly and infertile part of the region.

ACTIVITIES

1 Write a response giving your opinion of the Kanaks' system of land rights.

2 Investigate the early history of French colonisation. Find evidence to show how the Kanaks were treated by the French. Refer to pictures, diaries, and early newspaper reports. You can present this report in the form of a human rights document.

After French colonisation

The first Europeans to live in New Caledonia often married local Kanaks and lived on the outskirts of the fertile land. However, after a period of time the Europeans began to purchase land using barter and exchanging guns, axes, etc. The documents signed were not understood by the Kanaks who could not read French, or interpret French law. Given that under the traditional system it was not possible to 'buy' land, considerable misunderstanding developed between the Kanaks and the French about precisely what rights the Europeans had acquired.

France took possession of New Caledonia in 1853, and soon after the Governor declared that all land which was 'not occupied' belonged to the government. The government also had exclusive right to 'purchase land' which was 'occupied' by Kanaks. Soon after, in order to establish their colony in New Caledonia, early settlers were given plots of up to 100 hectares. This allocation of land forced the Kanaks into the less fertile mountain regions. In fact, until 1945, Kanaks were not allowed into Noumea, the capital of New Caledonia.

Fig. 50 The first French visitors to New Caledonia. If the Kanak people could re-write history, do you think the French would be welcomed as they were?

ACTIVITIES

1 Discuss in class the two systems of land distribution and ownership. How did they differ?

2 Write answers to these questions.

a What kind of misunderstandings would have occurred during these 'land sales'?

b Why were the Kanaks disadvantaged in the early exchanges of land?

c Why do you think the conflict occurred and what could have been done in the early stages to prevent it?

d What do you think may happen to a culture when its traditional way of life is severely disrupted?

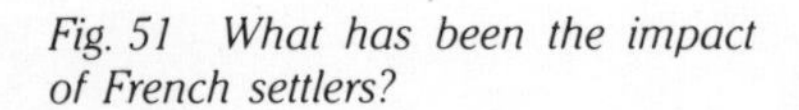

Fig. 51 What has been the impact of French settlers?

Land distribution

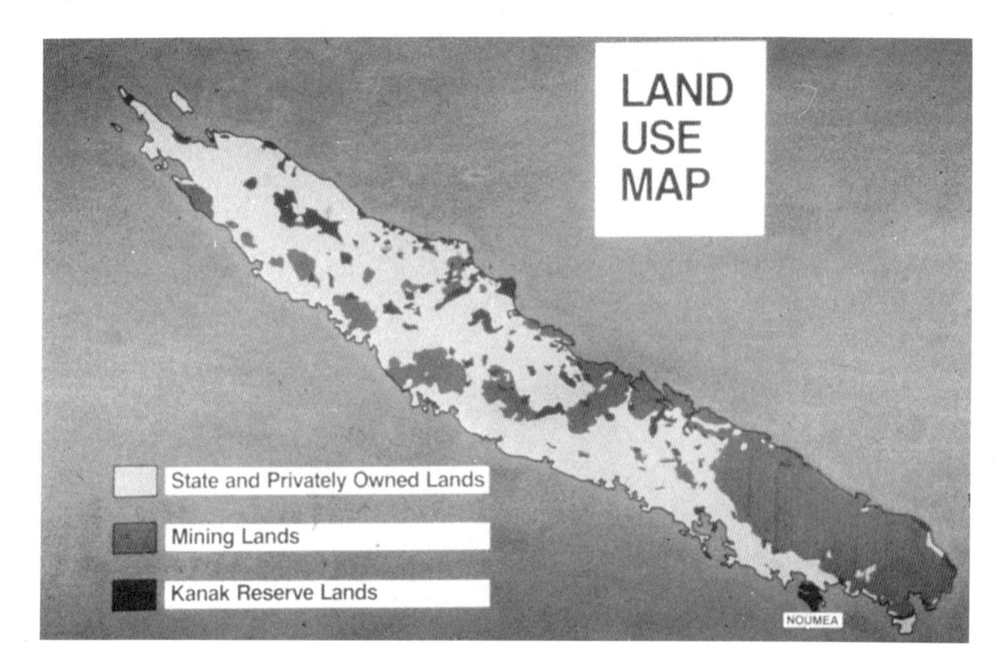

Fig. 52 Land use in New Caledonia. Describe the distribution of land use. Who benefits most?

Most of the island (prior to French occupation) was infertile and mountainous, unusable for traditional subsistence, so people lived in the narrow valleys and coastal plains. Though all cultivatable land was claimed by the Kanak people, the vast sterile lands were not, so that the population tended to be sparse and its density relatively high.

Fig. 53 Why were the Kanaks pushed into these valleys?

Most of the land in New Caledonia belongs to four per cent of non-indigenous owners who hold very large ranches of more than 2000 hectares. Fifty-two per cent of landowners have less than twenty-five hectares each. About 25 000 Kanaks (about 6000 families) have about 165 000 hectares on reserves and 12 000 hectares in private concessions.

The Kanak revolt

Fig. 54 French troops rounding up Kanaks after the rebellions. Why did the Kanaks rebel?

Compare the following two articles.

Article 1

In 1876 a new law created new boundaries for land occupied by the Kanak tribes. This new law took land away from the tribes to make it available for French settlers. This new law was one reason for the 1897 revolt in which over 1000 Kanaks were killed, their leaders taken and murdered. The Kanaks killed over 200 immigrants and over 200 hundred French stations were pillaged or destroyed in the revolt.

The French undertook reprisals and a bitter conflict broke out between the two groups. As the Kanaks were forced into the interior, their houses were burnt and their gardens destroyed. The French Government took land off any Kanak who challenged French occupation. The French, having much better military equipment, carried out extensive attacks on the Kanaks who disobeyed French law. Slowly, the best land was occupied by the French settlers while the Kanaks were sent to special reservations, often in the hills where it was more difficult to survive. The Kanaks soon learned the methods used by the French and they would flee their villages before the French attacked them. In the process, the majority of land was taken by the French settlers and the Kanaks were evicted. In 1860 the population of New Caledonia was 30 000. By 1891 the indigenous population had declined to 19 500.

Article 2

French launch hostage rescue

By MARY-LOUISE O'CALLAGHAN, Noumea, Monday

French troops tonight launched an operation to free 16 gendarmes held hostage and to neutralise Kanak separatists in New Caledonia.

The French Minister for Overseas Territories, Mr Bernard Pons, took a hard line against the separatists, saying: "We will use guns to fight guns. I have given instructions that all those who attack the armed forces will be neutralised."

The operation to release the hostages was announced despite a threat by militant Kanaks that a military effort would trigger a bloodbath.

Of the 27 gendarmes originally seized by Kanaks on Friday, 11 were freed this morning after local chiefs intervened to persuade the separatists to release them.

Mr Pons, announcing on local television the operation to free the remaining 16, said: "The Government will liberate the hostages as quickly as possible, arrest the kidnappers and bring them to justice.

"The operation will take place in the following hours and I think we will reach a result quickly . . . The Government cannot accept that one injures, one kills gendarmes, that one takes them hostage."

Sporadic fighting continued throughout the territory, including the Loyalty Islands, where 12 Kanaks were arrested this morning.

The first Kanak death occurred today when an 18-year-old woman was shot dead during fighting between separatists and gendarmes in the east-coast town of Canala, which has been cut off from the rest of the main island for nearly three days by barricades manned by armed and masked Kanaks.

More than 30 people, fearing reprisals from the separatists, are believed to have sought refuge in the town's police station this afternoon.

At Houailou, 50 kilometres to the north, a 17-year-old mixed-race youth from a loyalist family is not expected to live after being shot in the chest.

French settlers on the west coast set up their own roadblocks and patrols today after a couple trying to break a Kanak barricade were attacked with bush knives and axes but escaped with minor injuries.

Shortly before flying to Ouvea today to visit the 11 freed hostages, Mr Pons confirmed that France was ignoring FLNKS demands for negotiations on independence for New Caledonia.

The kidnappers had also demanded the cancellation of regional and French presidential elections yesterday. Results released today showed that the right-wing RPCR party, linked to the French Prime Minister, Mr Chirac, took control of all four regional assemblies. The FLNKS, which boycotted the elections, previously controlled three.

The RPCR won 35 of the 48 seats with the National Front party of the hard-line rightist Mr Jean-Marie Le Pen winning eight. The official turnout of 54 per cent was higher than the 50 per cent of four years ago.

REUTER reports from Paris that the FLNKS predicted yesterday that a bloodbath would follow any military attempt to free the gendarmes by force.

"By refusing to negotiate on a matter of such gravity, the French Government alone will bear responsibility for the bloodbath which will result from its operation," the Paris office of the FLNKS said in a statement.

The FLNKS accused the French authorities of repression on Ouvea, where they said Kanak men had been separated from women and children in the village of Gossanah and were being "tortured to reveal where the hostages are being held prisoner".

The FLNKS said gendarmes had dragged a separatist Kanak priest from his sickbed and had kept him tied to a tree outside an army encampment to force him to talk. In the village of Mouli, it said, French troops had ransacked homes and destroyed personal belongings.

The *Age*

ACTIVITIES

1 Organise the class into three different groups. Group two has arrived from France to settle in New Caledonia. The Kanaks strongly resist giving up their traditional land for the new settlers. What issues are raised by all three groups and how could the situation be approached? What are the problems? Each group should present their particular point of view and try to come to some resolution. When the role-play is finished discuss in class the questions which follow.

Group 1 represents a Kanak tribe. From the information you have learnt about the Kanak culture, divide yourself into a clan living in a certain village. Organise your land so that each member has enough to live on and elect a chief. You have been on this land for many generations. On a large piece of paper draw the map of your village, showing the distribution of land. You are not familiar with the European way of life and do not write French.

Group 2 represents the French settlers. You have arrived from France to settle in New Caledonia after reading about the life there. The French government says you are able to take land from the Kanaks so you are expecting to be given land when you arrive. You know nothing about the Kanaks. You are preparing for your new life, designing your farm and deciding on the type of land you want. You are very enthusiastic.

Group 3 represents the French Governor and police. Your job is to allocate land to the new settlers. You do this in many ways using money, barter, and offering alternative land. You are under a lot of pressure from the French government to take over good land and settle the new immigrants. You decide to negotiate for land from the Kanak tribe. The French law allows you to do this.

a What were the main issues involved in this conflict?

b Were the three groups able to come to any resolution?

2 Imagine you are a Kanak community leader in New Caledonia delivering a speech on how the French have responded to your calls for independence. Write and deliver your speech to the class.

Politics before French colonisation

The main Kanak political structure was the clan. Clans or villages were, most of the time, federated under the authority of a chiefly system. The chief was above all a political leader, the master of peace and war, though he was often also a war chief. Very frequently chiefs were not among the large landowners of the tribe. In fact, some were almost landless and dependent on lands made available by landowners in the local area.

Political power was always separate from power over land although the chief often negotiated with the colonialists when purchases of land were made. Kanak

Fig. 55 Famous Kanak Chief Mindia Néja in 1878, 1892, and 1912. Describe how his dress reflects the changes to the island.

political decision-making operates through consensus, a process whereby individual positions are merged into a collective one.

Politics after French colonisation

From 1853 until January 1860, New Caledonia was a dependency of the 'French settlements in Oceania' controlled by a governor in Tahiti selected from Paris. Then, in 1860, the administration of the colony was placed under the direction of a local governor, assisted by a Consultative Council, managed and run by the French settlers.

In 1885, the General Council with sixteen members was established. For the first time, this executive authority was responsible for certain areas which were previously under control of the State (management of heritage, road system, public works, social assistance). This system continued until 1940 when the French created indigenous districts divided into tribes led by chiefs who were appointed by the French Government.

ACTIVITY

Discuss in class in what ways the French and the Kanak political systems differed and how the two systems operated.

Fig. 56 Why did the French missionaries come to New Caledonia?

Conflicting reports

Read, assess and compare these articles and photographs (Figs 57 & 58).

Article 1

Up until 1946, Kanaks did not have the right to leave the reserves which the [French] colonial administration had forced them into, without police permission. Until 1946, there was, on the one side, the white society of settlers in charge of all the political and economic affairs of the country, and on the other side, the Kanak society slowly dying in the reserves created specifically to allow the Kanaks to 'die in peace'.

Dewe Gorodey, Kanak activist

Article 2

Everyone is free to have his/her own opinion and to express it, within the framework of democratic debate, as long as he/she does not go against the law, or commit offences punishable by law. Everyone is free to go wherever he/she pleases.

Bernard Pons, French State Secretary for the Overseas Departments and Territories, 1987

Article 3

Today under the French colonial rule the Kanak people are not at all represented in the essential jobs required to run a National State. After 123 years of this French rule, since 1853 we have . . . no lawyers, no economists, no engineers. The education system does not allow the Kanak people to acquire these skills, today there are only seven Kanaks who have university degrees and we have only one secondary school teacher.

Dewe Gorodey, Kanak activist

Fig. 57 Graffiti on walls in villages highlights Kanak feelings. What is this message trying to say?

Article 4

New Caledonia . . . is probably the last non-independent tropical territory in the world where a country can get its subjects to migrate. Thus it is necessary to seize this last chance to create another French-speaking country . . . the French presence . . . can only be threatened by nationalist claims made by the indigenous people [Kanaks], supported by allies from other Pacific countries.

In the short- to medium-term the massive immigration of metropolitan French or citizens from overseas departments . . . should enable this danger to be averted by immediately improving the numerical balance of the races.

A letter written in 1972 by the French Prime Minister to the Minister of Overseas Territories about New Caledonia

Fig. 58 Confrontation between the French troops and Kanaks has resulted in an increased armed presence on the island. Where would these personnel come from?

ACTIVITIES

1 You be the judge. After reading and viewing all the articles, write a front page headline article about life in New Caledonia. What impression would you give?

2 Discuss in class the ways in which the French settlers maintain control in New Caledonia.

3 Write answers to these questions.

a How have the French nationals involved or not involved the Kanaks in governing New Caledonia?

b In what ways can the Kanaks gain some influence in the decision-making process in New Caledonia?

c What do you think is the attitude of French nationals towards New Caledonia?

4 Why do you think Kanaks write on walls? Draw some of your own political graffiti about an issue which concerns you. What would you write and how would you design it?

Recent events in New Caledonia

Two main political groups have emerged in New Caledonia. The Kanak Socialist National Liberation Front (FLNKS) brings together five parties. Its President was Jean-Marie Tjibaou, leader of the Front's largest party, Union Caledonniene, until his assassination in May, 1989.

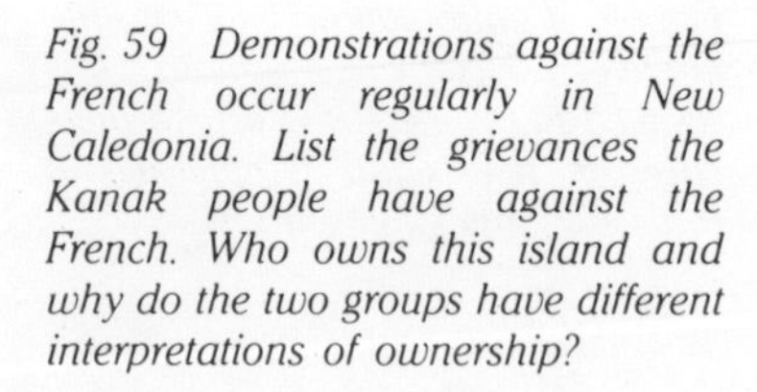

Fig. 59 Demonstrations against the French occur regularly in New Caledonia. List the grievances the Kanak people have against the French. Who owns this island and why do the two groups have different interpretations of ownership?

Fig. 60 Kanak roadblocks in the country disrupt the movement of French troops in outlying areas. How does this influence normal life throughout the island? Can you think of a solution to this conflict?

> Our struggle against [the] French Government in New Caledonia started in 1969. The four different groups of young Kanak activists came together in January 1976 to form a Provisional Bureau which prepared the platform of the Kanak Liberation Party [now the FLNKS] with the help of the people. Our struggle against [the] French Government is the logical result of its policy of oppression and exploitation towards our people since 1853. The Kanak Liberation Party is a widely based party of Kanak people, with the majority of members being young men and women. The most important function of the [Front] is political education of our people. (Dewe Gorodey)

The Rally For New Caledonia Within the Republic (RPCR) is made up of five parties. Its leader is Jacques Lafleur. This is a group who do not want independence and oppose autonomy. They want the French to stay in New Caledonia because French money provides jobs and the police protect the white settlers. They fear that if the Kanaks take control they will lose all their wealth, property and political dominance.

Fig. 61 French caloches or cowboys in New Caledonia. What would these people do?

Fig. 62 A caloche's house. Is there unequal distribution of wealth?

Although some elements of this group are armed and have threatened a bloodbath if moves are made towards independence, such an event could be contained swiftly by the strong French military presence in the territory.

Facing international pressure to grant self-determination to New Caledonia, the French Government prepared for a referendum to ask the Kanaks and French settlers whether or not they wanted to be independent. In 1988, the referendum was held in New Caledonia but the two major parties split on the vote and the Kanaks decided to boycott the plebiscite.

Continuing conflict

Read these three newspaper articles and answer the following questions.

Article 1

Kanaks step up anti-poll violence

Agence France Presse

NOUMEA: Widespread violence flared yesterday in New Caledonia as Kanak separatists sniped at gendarmes and erected roadblocks in a bid to disrupt presidential and regional elections.

At least seven gendarmes were injured yesterday in violence across the French South Pacific territory, police said.

One gendarme was seriously wounded in an exchange of fire with Kanaks who staged an ambush near the town hall at Canala on the east coast of La Grande Terre, New Caledonia's main island, police said.

An explosion in Canala left five gendarmes injured, police said. They were taken to hospital in Noumea.

Another gendarme was slightly wounded by a gunshot while on patrol near a security forces camp at Pouembout on the west coast, they said.

Gendarmes traded shots with armed separatists on the land of the turbulent Saint Louis tribe about 15 kilometres south of Noumea, they added.

In other incidents, security forces were fired on while on patrol near Kone and Paita on the west coast.

POLLING booths in New Caledonia, where regional elections were being conducted at the same time as the presidential poll in France, closed yesterday.

In the local poll, the pro-Chirac RPCR (Rally for Caledonia in the Republic) won an absolute majority of 35 out of a total of 48 in the local legislative assembly.

The extreme right-wing National Front won eight seats.

Officials in New Caledonia said the turnout there was "of the same order" as the 60 per cent obtained in a referendum on self-determination held last September.

Agence France Presse

Armed Kanaks, some wearing hoods to avoid identification, blocked roads with tree trunks. The roadblocks were mainly near Canala and the offshore Loyalty Islands, where the situation was reported to be especially tense.

State-run radio broadcast a report that the police station on the island of Mare in the Loyalty group had been attacked by armed Kanaks. But there was no official confirmation of this report.

Meanwhile, the separatist Kanak Socialist National Liberation Front (FLNKS) claimed responsibility for the seizure of 27 gendarmes on Friday on the island of Ouvea in the Loyalty group.

The 27 gendarmes were captured by Kanak militants in a surprise raid in which three gendarmes were hacked to death and two were seriously wounded.

The militants, who have split up into several groups and hidden in the bush, demanded the cancellation of the regional elections as one condition for the release of their captives.

The FLNKS politburo said in a statement released yesterday that the operation was not an isolated action by a few extremists.

The hostage-taking was part of the strategy decided on at an FLNKS congress in February aimed at overturning the French Government's latest statute for the troubled South Pacific territory, the statement said.

The FLNKS urged the Kanak people to "strengthen its mobilisation" throughout New Caledonia and blamed the crisis on Minister for Overseas Territories Bernard Pons and Jacques Lafleur, the leader of

The anti-Independence Rally for Caledonia in the (French) Republic Party (RPCR).

Mr Pons was scheduled to arrive in Noumea later yesterday on an urgent mission to New Caledonia following the seizure of the Ouvea gendarmes.

In another reaction to the hostage-taking further reinforcements for the security forces arrived from France yesterday, police said.

The new arrivals totalled 160 men, including about 20 gendarmes belonging to the elite GIGN intervention squad.

A heavy voter turnout was reported in the territorial capital of Noumea where the situation was quiet.

The French High Commission said 101 out of 139 polling stations throughout the territory had opened normally. Only seven polling stations had to be closed in the south (Noumea) and west of the main island. But on the east coast and in the Loyalty Islands where the Kanak population is in the majority 31 out of 57 polling stations remained closed.

Informed sources said the authorities had decided not to open certain polling stations in remote districts in order to avoid any further risk of gendarmes being snatched as hostages.

A total of 87,353 New Caledonian electors were eligible to vote in the election for a new French president and to choose 48 councillors for the territory's newly-delimited four regions.

The FLNKS, which took part in the local government under the previous statute, has called on its supporters to boycott the regional election and oppose the new statute for the territory enacted by the Government of Prime Minister Jacques Chirac in December.

South China Morning Post

Article 2

"Colonial" situation must end, says minister

The newly appointed French Minister for Overseas Territories and Departments, Olivier Stirn has said the French government must first put an end to "the colonial situation in New Caledonia".

Mr Stirn, who served as Overseas Territories Minister in the mid-1970s for the centre/right government of Raymond Barre, told *l'Ouest-France* newspaper that the so-called Pons statute of autonomy enacted by the Chirac government should be scrapped. He said the French government might introduce land and tax changes in the territory, but that long-term action would await the report of the mission currently in the territory.

The new French Minister for Defence, Jean-Pierre Chevenement, has ordered an inquiry into the killing of 19 Kanaks on Ouvea Island early this month during a military attack to free 23 French hostages held by Kanak militants on Ouvea.

Kanaks say that three militants and one village youth who brought food to the hostages were killed by the military after surrender. Testimony from a Kanak gendarme and a member of the elite Gendarme Intervention Squad (GIGN) appears to support this claim.

As the inquiry began the French daily *le Monde* quoted from a report by GIGN Captain Legorjus that the former Overseas Territories Minister Bernard Pons had considered using napalm and heavy artillery to end the hostage drama, and had stopped negotiations with the Kanaks.

Chevenement also has ordered an inquiry into the shooting at Touho and stressed to the armed forces that they have no role in maintaining civil law and order.

Pacific Report

Article 3

Respect Kanaks, says Paris MP

By MARGARET MURRAY, Paris, Sunday

A leading French Socialist parliamentarian, Mr Georges Lemoine, said today after returning from his first visit to New Caledonia in two years, that France "must stop humiliating Kanak leaders".

Mr Lemoine, Mayor of Chartres and State Secretary for Overseas Territories in the former Socialist Government, has formed an association in France to seek a peaceful solution in New Caledonia.

He told 'Le Monde': "I am more worried than ever, as are all those in the territory in charge of the Kanak community."

During the visit he was told that a Kanak leader, Yeweini Yeweini, was stripped and searched in humiliating circumstances at the airport on his return from Paris, and several Kanak leaders had told Mr Lemoine that his next visit would be to their graves.

Although Mr Lemoine regarded such words as emotive and pessimistic, he nevertheless said they showed a determination which, given the spirit behind the FLNKS and the ideals of independence among the young, France must take into account.

He said the referendum in New Caledonia last September brought neither answers to everyone's questions nor conditions for discussions between the French and Kanak communities. His main impression was the division between them: one thought history had stopped and there were no more problems; and the Kanaks believed the future was theirs and they must go beyond the framework of French institutions.

For France, Mr Lemoine said, the main problem was to know under what conditions France could stay in the Pacific. New Caledonia should not be a pawn in French electoral games, he said. He shared the view of many centrists who regretted that regional elections there would be on 24 April, the same day as the first round of French presidential elections.

The FLNKS will boycott the elections "to be in the best position to negotiate with the new President or the new Government on conditions for a real referendum on self-determination leading to independence".

President Mitterrand, expected to be the Socialist presidential candidate again, said last week that it was in the interests of France and New Caledonia to "step out of the logic of confrontation between the two communities and not to seek to establish the supremacy of one over the other".

The *Age*

1 Who put out the report in the first article? What point of view is it taking?

2 Why were the Kanaks boycotting the election?

3 What is the colonial situation Mr Olivier Stirn refers to in the second article?

4 Explain the conflicting reports about the death of Kanaks on the island of Ouvea.

New Caledonia today

Read and compare the following five articles and Fig. 63 (page 96).

Article 1

For the young, life on the reserves is often boring. The individualism of the liberal industrial society offers a less constraining alternative, so many of them want to leave the reserves, with their long, monotonous days, tension between families, and social life dominated by the elders. Many young Melanesians reject the traditional system of the reserves in the name of progress and modernisation and want to integrate into the industrial society.

Article 2

The most common pattern for New Caledonians is to spend most of their working life in the towns where the industry is situated. Thus, for many New Caledonians, the reserve provides a sense of well-being, a place where one goes for holidays or weekends, and an escape from the pressures of European civilisation.

Article 3

> The attitude of the French towards the Kanak people is one of racism and paternalism. As such there are great social problems like unemployment and alcoholism, concerning our culture. But now they have discovered they can make money out of Kanak culture, so they have exploited it for tourism. They have not done anything to involve the people in the running of their country.
>
> *Dewe Gorodey, Kanak activist*

Article 4

Continuing tension hampers efforts to establish dialogue in New Caledonia

Tension remains high in New Caledonia as the territory goes through another period of 'wait and see' on its political future.

As the mission sent by France to renew dialogue with the independence movement began talks in Noumea a Kanak youth was killed by an army patrol at Touho on the east coast. The youth was one of two guarding the entrance to the Paola tribal village when confronted by an army patrol at night.

The army said the Kanaks were armed and that a soldier fired in self-defence, while Kanak witnesses said the youth was unarmed and was shot in the back as he ran away.

The incident reflects the nervousness in the territory, with Kanaks, settlers and military all operating on respective self-defence footings.

Pacific Report

Article 5

> The tragic murders of Kanak leaders Jean-Marie Tjibaou and Yeiwene Yeiwene on May 4 1989 mark a significant turning point in the campaign for independence from France.
>
> Tjibaou played a dynamic and charismatic role as a leader, as mayor of the town of Hienghene in the north of Kanaky, as leader of the Union Caledonniene, the largest party in the Kanak Socialist Liberation Front (FLNKS), as president of the independence movement and as an international figure and diplomat and negotiator with France, the South Pacific and the United Nations.
>
> He was largely responsible for the Matignon Accord, an agreement signed in 1988 with the French government and Jacques Lafleur, the right-wing leader of the Caldoche settler community. This agreement promised one rule of direct government from France, followed by elections for three provisional councils which would allow a measure of self-government and local administration. After a ten year transition period, there would be a vote on independence in 1998.
>
> *'Kanaky After Tjibaou?'* Pacific Issues, *1989*

EXTRACT 13.5

The charter of the FLNKS

This Charter aims to spell out the objectives of the Kanak people, to explain why and how they are conducting a national liberation struggle so that their rights may triumph.

It has been reaffirmed throughout the continuity of resistance of the Kanak people for over 130 years, that there will be a defined period of national liberation struggle, a transitory period, in preparation for Kanak and socialist independence.

Why the national liberation struggle

1. Declaring:
(a) That the French government is a firm accomplice of the colonial situation, which it maintains;
(b) That Francois Mitterrand, who became president of the Republic by the mandate of May 10, 1981, has not kept to his commitments;
(c) That the declarations of Nainville-les-Roches on our innate and active right to independence have effectively not been put into practice;
(d) That the French government, rejecting all the measures proposed by the Independence Front to prepare the steps to Kanak and socialist independence,
- Is imposing on us the Lemoine statute with all its restrictions (election to the Territorial Assembly, State-Territory Committee, referendum in 1989, etc)
- Is directly threatening the Kanak people with the prospect of disappearing, by decisively making it a minority in its own land;

(e) That capitalist and imperialist exploitation by economic interests foreign to our country, is being continued to the profit of colonial France and to that of its allies;
(f) That the French government pursues an immigration policy which aims at,
- preventing control over the economy by the Kanak people
- forbidding this people the full exercise of its right to work
- striking at its integrity and at its social, cultural and political unity;

(g) That the French government is putting in place legal and military structures to repress the Kanak forces working for Kanak and socialist independence;

The Independence Front has judged that the Kanak people are entering a phase of struggle for Kanak independence: the liberation struggle.

Because of this, the Independence Front has decided to break off its dialogue with the French government, to dissolve itself, and to participate together with all the living forces of the independence movement in setting up a Kanak Socialist National Liberation Front.

2. We affirm the existence of the Kanak people, proudly attached to its cultural identity and to its own customary values.
3. We demand the legitimate and inalienable rights of the Kanak people, for since the 24th of September 1853 France has ignored this people's rights and has taken them away, unilaterally installing its colonial laws and system, a source of institutional violence in respect to the Kanaks.
4. The sacred and inalienable rights of the Kanak people, oppressed and injured by the colonial situation, are the following (see U.N. declarations 1514 and 2621):
(a) the right to be recognised as a single people;
(b) the right to dignity and freedom;
(c) the right to be considered as the only legitimate people in the Kanak land and to have there their own homeland;
(d) the right to practice self-determination;
(e) the right to obtain restoration of all the lands so as to set up the Kanak country as an integral whole;
(f) the right to the immediate exercise, without conditions or reservations, of their own sovereignty which will allow them to freely choose their political system: Kanak and socialist independence;
(g) the right to the necessary means to pursue their economic, social and cultural development in order to build socialism;
(h) the right to make welcome the non-Kanaks.

The Kanak Socialist National Liberation Front

1. *Character.* The Kanak people are alone responsible for their fight for national liberation. To best lead this struggle, they need an effective force: the FLNKS.
2. *Composition.* All the signatories to this Charter: Kanak independence fighters and anti-colonialist non-Kanaks, organisations, unions, movements, associations, churches . . . making up the FLNKS, are its active members.
3. *Role.* The national liberation struggle is universal: it goes on at every level at the same time. The FLNKS is therefore the union of the living forces which have as their goal the achievement of Kanak socialist independence. That is to say, a Liberation Front for freeing the Kanak land of colonialism, capitalism and imperialism, with the aim of setting up a socialism based on the local reality, but which will itself be defined in the course of the struggle by the fighters for liberty.
4. *Organisation.* Leading the FLNKS and co-ordination among its members is the job of the Political Bureau. This political nucleus will propose the line of conduct which will then be put to plenary meetings of the FLNKS.
5. *Strategy.* This will be worked out in the course of the struggle:
(a) It is a single and universal strategy;
(b) It is directed first and foremost against the colonial oppressor, the French colonial power;
(c) It denounces the false colonial "democracy", and will boycott every coming election held in this framework;
(d) It is equally directed against both capitalism and imperialism, and aims to install a more just and socialist society;
(e) It aims to step-by-step establish Kanak laws and principles, in this territory, by concrete operations which demonstrate its own rights as opposed to the colonial authority.

An appeal for a commitment

1. The FLNKS launches an appeal to the non-Kanaks. They must recognise the legitimacy of the Kanak people and support their national liberation struggle, so as to contribute to its success. Only such a commitment of solidarity in the liberation struggle will guarantee their future citizenship in the country of Kanak and socialist independence.
2. The FLNKS appeals to the brother countries of the Pacific and similarly to all those countries which have voted for declarations 1514 and 2621 of the United Nations, to lend their help and support to the struggle of the Kanak people.
3. It is urgent for Kanaks to get together and organise to win freedom. The first act of this commitment is for each to sign this Charter for the liberation struggle.

Fig. 63 FLNKS Charter. What are the objectives of the FLNKS and how does it seek to resolve the conflict?

ACTIVITIES

1 Discuss in class the main reasons for the continuing conflict.

2 Write answers to these questions.

a What do you think are some of the long-term solutions to these problems? List them and discuss them together in class.

b Evaluate the Matignon Accord. What are its advantages and disadvantages?

c How do the main points in the FLNKS Charter differ from the French position?

RESEARCH PROJECT

1 Write an essay which considers what the main problems are when two cultures live together with different value systems and beliefs. How can these problems be replaced by more cooperative living? Should one culture or ethnic group get more rights than another?

2 Research other countries in the world which are still administered by foreign powers. Many ex-colonies are now today's Third World or poorer nations. Why do you think this has happened?

Resources

Brooks, M. & Codrington, S. *Australia's Pacific Neighbours*, Action for World Development and the Geography Teachers' Association, NSW, 1989.

Dornoy, M. *Politics in New Caledonia*, Sydney University Press, 1984.

Frazer, H. (ed.) *Pacific Report*, no. 5, Canberra, 1988.

Frazer, H. *New Caledonia*, Peace Research Centre, Research School of Pacific Studies, Australian National University, Canberra, 1988.

'Kanaky After Tjibaou?' *Pacific Issues*, Peace and Social Justice Committee, Uniting Church of Australia, Melbourne, 1989.

Kircher, I. *The Kanaks of New Caledonia*, The Minority Rights Group Report, no. 71, Minority Rights Group Ltd, 1986.

Presence New Caledonia, bulletin of the French Embassy, no. 5, 3rd Quarter, 1987.

Saussol, A. *Land and Identity in New Caledonia*, a review by R. Crocombe in *Pacific Identity*, a special issue of *Pacific Perspective* (vol. 12, no. 2), South Pacific Social Sciences Association, Box 5083, Raiwaqa, Fiji.

'The Kanak Movement', an interview with Dewe Gorodey in Woods, G. (ed.) *South Pacific Dossier*, Australian Council for Overseas Aid, Canberra, 1978.

6 Navigation as a Cultural Tradition

Focus question

What impact does European culture have on the oral navigation tradition in the Pacific?

▲▲▲ Related questions ▲▲▲

1 What is an oral tradition?

2 What is the important knowledge which is passed down between generations?

3 How does the oral navigation tradition (hatag) work?

4 How is the navigation system a part of Pacific Island culture?

5 In what ways could the European system of navigation, with its technology, change the status of navigators in the Islands?

6 How did the Europeans view the Islanders' oral tradition?

Navigators of Micronesia

Imagine being in a small canoe somewhere in Micronesia without any modern scientific navigational aids to assist you. There are thousands of atolls and islands so how would you know where to go, where the winds were blowing and which way the tides were moving?

After drifting for two days, a Micronesian navigator in a small out-rigger canoe picks you up. While you recover, you notice that the navigator has no aids or maps, not even a compass. Still, he is able to take you to a small, inhabited island two days voyage away.

Traditional navigators from Micronesia use no external devices (like compasses) when they navigate long distances. They have been doing this since their early history.

The Pacific Island navigator has a high status in the village. A navigator's knowledge and understanding of the sea gives him considerable importance. Whoever commands the out-rigger canoes has power in the society because everyone else is reliant on the navigators for all communication between the islands. Only a handful of men ever become master navigators and young men are discouraged from taking it on because so many fail.

Women also play an important role in navigation. Although they do not navigate themselves, they have considerable understanding of what is involved. They also keep a check on the condition of the out-riggers and the navigators in order to maintain safety standards.

Fig. 64 A Fijian out-rigger of the late eighteenth century. Why was an out-rigger important to the life and economy of the island groups? (After T. Williams, 1858.)

ACTIVITY

In Micronesian society, knowledge and information about the seas and stars gives the navigator power and status. In Western society, which professions have status and power? Where does their power come from? How is it maintained? You can use these questions as the basis for a class discussion.

Role of navigation in Micronesian culture

Navigation is just not about sailing a canoe from one island to another. It is an integral part of Micronesian culture. Each navigator undergoes long formal training, just like people in any society, before entering positions of power and responsibility. A main difference between Western and Micronesian teaching is that knowledge is oral and not written down.

The young navigator must remember all the information, including details of star courses, without writing it down. Navigators develop the ability to remember hundreds of voyages including knowledge about the currents, birds, tides, ocean colour and weather.

Comparing oral and literate societies

There are a number of significant differences between the approach to learning in a literate society and in an oral society. Read the following extract and think about these differences before doing the activities.

Literate societies

1. Success–failure image: begins with early literacy experience in school.
2. Law: rules for social organisation and conduct codified by specialists in . . . jargon
3. History: documented, presented as fact, formal subject of study in school, very limited data on minority cultures, disconnected from living past . . .
4. Information storage: data books, files, archives, libraries; memory is suspect.
5. Literature: stories are 'heard' through print; great literature is read only in school setting.
6. Logical, analytic, linear thinking, taught in schools and held as the perfect model.

Non-literate or oral societies

1. Each individual has an appropriate place in the system, even if a hierarchical one.
2. Custom: rules for social organisation and conduct known and understood by all, arbitrated by [village leaders].
3. Legend: reposed in human memory of [chosen] individuals, rich in data, connected with living past through oral transmission.
4. Memory storage: select individuals are [storers] of information; memory is honoured and developed.
5. Oralature: stories are told to living audiences; great epics are preserved and transmitted by popular demand.
6. Wholistic [approach]: less concern with analysis of parts, but rather how they work together, [looking at the whole thing, not just the parts].

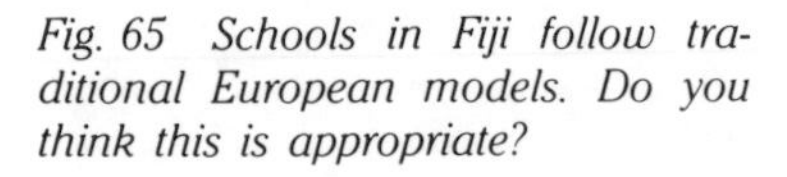

Fig. 65 Schools in Fiji follow traditional European models. Do you think this is appropriate?

ACTIVITIES

1 From the two lists opposite, select what you think are the most important things to learn and write them out in order of importance. What could you incorporate from the oral tradition into your own school?

2 Discuss what you think are the advantages of an oral tradition.

3 Write answers to these questions.

- **a** In an oral tradition, how is information handed down and in what form?
- **b** How would school within an oral tradition be different from one within a written tradition?
- **c** What are the disadvantages of an oral teaching?
- **d** Why do you think the Micronesian navigators use an oral form of knowledge?
- **e** Why do Europeans find an oral tradition difficult to understand?
- **f** How would an oral tradition help maintain stability in society for thousands of years?

4 One student writes down how to get to a location in your town (try to use as many visual images as possible). The student whispers the directions to his or her neighbour who then passes it on to the next person until the whole class has, one by one, passed on the instruction. The last student to receive the instruction tells the rest of the class the final version. Then use the following questions as the basis for a class discussion.

- **a** How were the final instructions different from the original?
- **b** What is easy to remember and what is difficult?

Passing down knowledge

Like the Micronesian navigators, all societies believe there is certain knowledge that is important enough to pass on to the next generation.

For example, knowledge about navigation is extremely important for Pacific Island cultures and this knowledge is often passed down by relatives. Having knowledge gives those who use it certain power in society.

ACTIVITIES

1 List the things you believe are most important to know in order to survive in society. This could be placed in a time capsule for the next generation.

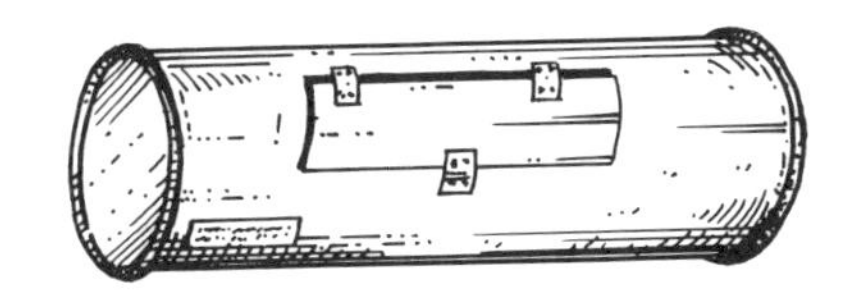

Fig. 66 A time capsule.

2 What would you write for the next generation to explain issues like:

- ▲ the meaning of life
- ▲ death
- ▲ where humans came from

The answers to these questions would also be put into your time capsule.

3 Imagine you are living in a society which has an oral tradition. Try to write a story about something which is 'not accepted' in your society. The story will help to educate the rest of the community not to indulge in things. For example, it could be about:

- ▲ greed
- ▲ deceit
- ▲ stealing

The art of memory

In an oral tradition factual information has to be learned and committed to memory. A navigator must also learn about the stars and how they rise and set along the horizon. In order to remember this information, much of it is told in the form of a story because stories are easier to remember than a string of facts. These stories often relate to Pacific Island cultural beliefs.

In early Greece, the orators (people who spoke publicly) used to learn all their speeches by memory. They would then develop a filing system in their minds by imagining large buildings with many rooms. In each room they would place

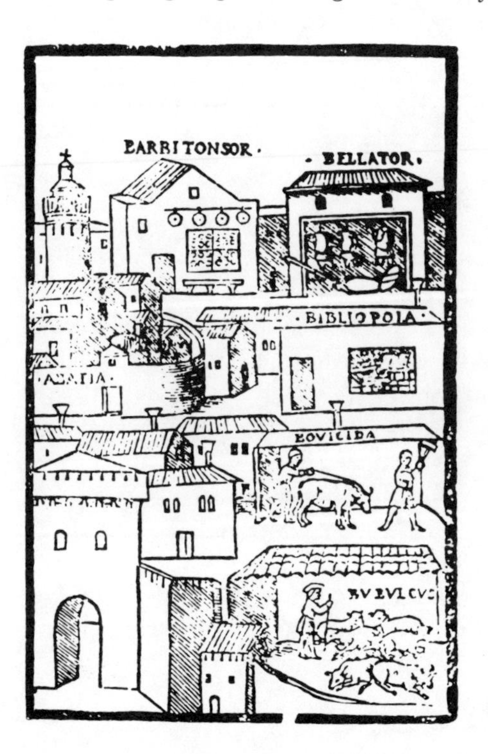

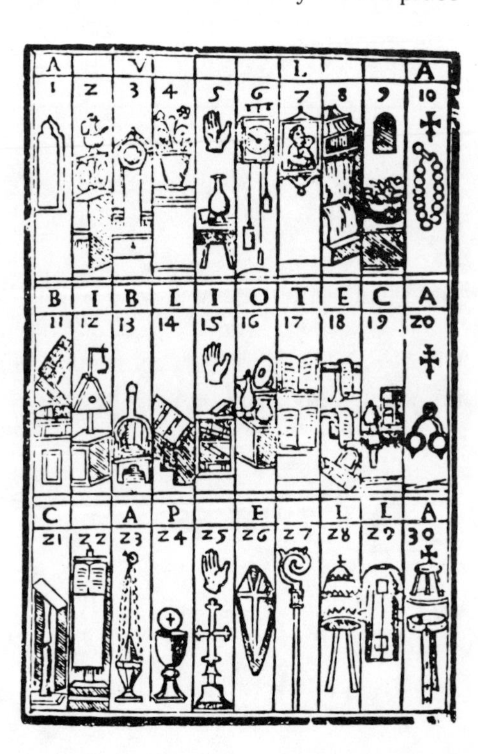

Fig. 67 Diagrams used to train the memory in sixteenth century Europe. What does it also tell us about life at this time?

a speech they had learned. When the time came to give a speech they would remember where they placed it in the building they had constructed in their minds, and once found, they would recall the speech.

The navigators developed the ability to remember large amounts of information. This was needed for their long journeys. The preservation and accuracy of an oral way of teaching demands an accurate memory. The students learn various techniques to aid the human memory. These are called 'mnemonic devices'.

Learning in groups also helps one another check the accuracy of details. Some members of a village had a special responsibility of remembering all the important details. Fear of offending gods or ancestors also helped ensure people did not forget the details. When sailing, an accurate memory could mean the difference between life and death.

ACTIVITIES

1 Design your own building and allocate rooms and other areas to store at least seven pieces or more of information. Try to memorise the diagram then give it to another student. Wait a few minutes and see if you can describe in detail where the material is stored. Try to do this by imagining you are going on a tour in the building.

2 Do you think you can learn to remember more information through symbols rather than the written word? Can you give any examples?

3 Computers are taking over many functions in our society, especially storing large quantities of information in data bases. Do you think our ability to remember is being reduced? If so, what will happen in the future? Compare this to the navigator's oral tradition which determines the role, behaviour and lifestyle of the community.

Training to be a navigator

The training is done on both sea and land. The student must acquire skills in steering, identifying different sea birds, how an out-rigger canoe handles, how fast it travels in different conditions, how it drifts when its sails are down, and the difference between canoe types.

Provisions for a long voyage

The staple diet for a long voyage usually included precooked fermented breadfruit, pounded taro, drinking and eating coconuts and baked fish. Any fish caught at sea was eaten raw or cooked on the boat. The carrying capacity of the big voyager canoes was enormous.

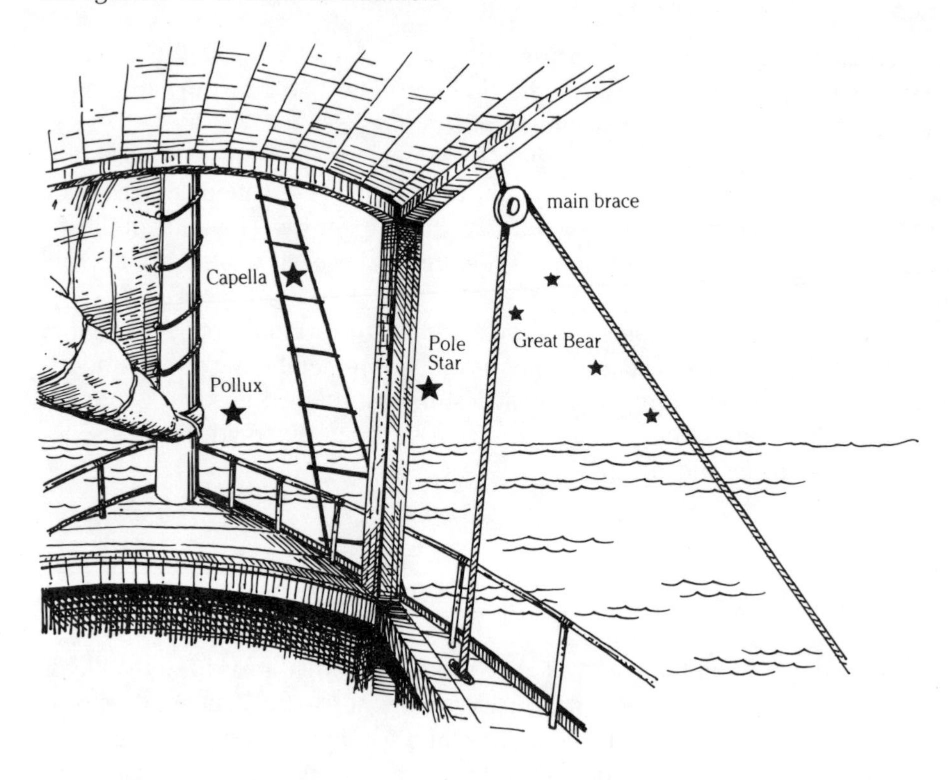

Fig. 68 Steering stars from Pulawat to Pikelot. What problems would result from using this method of navigation in the tropics?

A voyage from Woleai to Olimarao

The following account has been adapted from *Unwritten Knowledge* (see 'Resources' below).

Woleai in Micronesia is 188 kilometres away from Olimarao. The sailing directions which have been learned along with the star course include making suitable allowance for currents. The out-rigger sailing canoe sets out late in the afternoon, lining up astern two marks on shore that have been chosen for voyage on this course.

As the island disappears below the horizon a couple of hours later, the main way of keeping on course is by sailing at a constant angle to the wind and waves (which are usually felt rather than seen, and thus equally well at night). In another two hours, as dusk approaches, the navigator checks his course by the return of birds to Woleai. During the night (at a time depending on the time of year) Aldebaran [the star] rises over the bow to give yet another check. In fact, that particular star need not be seen, as the navigators know by name a whole succession of stars rising in approximately the same position.

Within range of about 40 kilometres, patterns or colours of clouds over islands indicate their position. The navigator might also note the deep phosphorescence which is like underwater lightning flashing in the direction indicating land.

During the voyage from Woleai to Olimarao the navigator focuses on the exact position of the canoe at all times in relation to known islands of the archipelago. He also imagines an island which is called 'etak' on the horizon.

By imagining the position of 'etak', the navigator moves under a succession of principal star directions to his destination.

Fig. 69 What role do atolls play in planning a voyage? What difficulties would traditional craft and sailors experience in finding these atolls? Why?

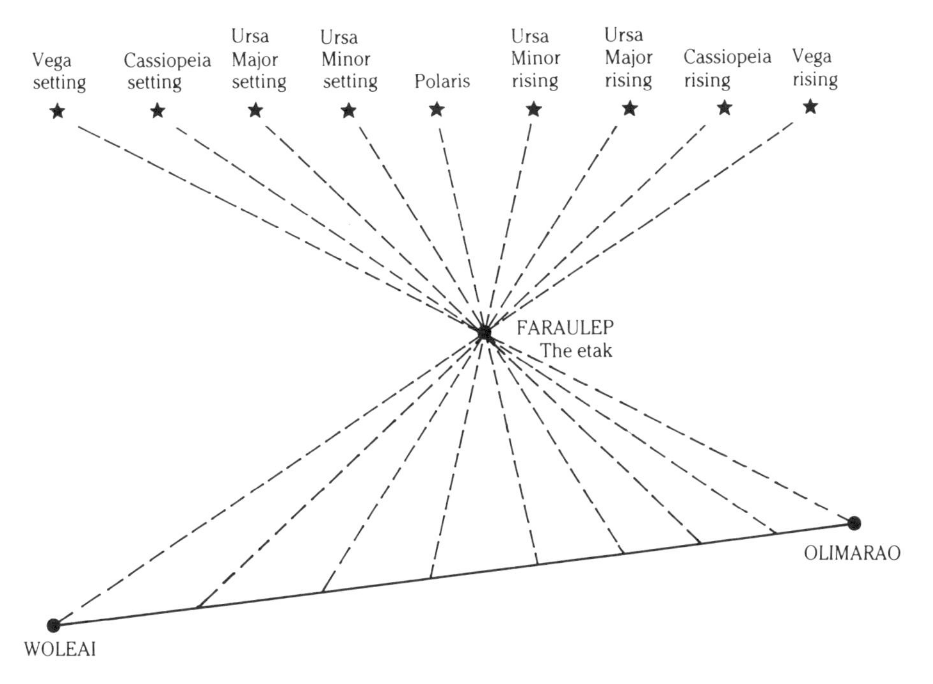

Fig. 70 Using the stars to guide the passage from Woleai to Olimarao. Why is this skill relied on less today? What tools are now used to increase the accuracy of navigation?

The navigators use both the clouds and water swells to keep their course. When there is limited visibility, watching the swells may be the only way to navigate. This is done by watching their effect on the out-rigger canoes. Navigators learn to understand about waves and swells through their stories. As long as the navigator remembers the key words or images, he will be able to relate it back to the swells and tides.

On longer voyages other techniques are used which include noticing subtle changes of sea colour at fixed locations over reefs and recognising the different types of sea life near the islands.

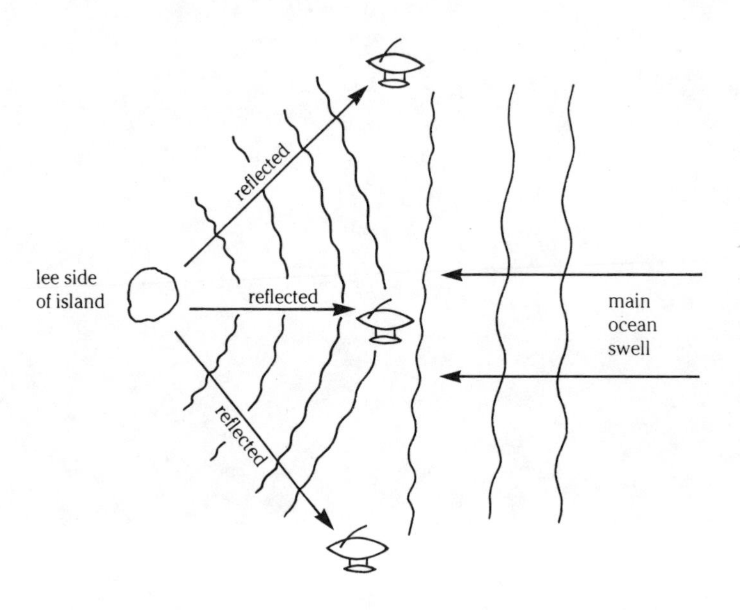

Fig. 71 Swell interference patterns. What does this swell interference indicate and why is it important to the navigators?

ACTIVITIES

1 Write answers to these questions.

- **a** Explain how the navigator keeps his course.
- **b** List some of the skills used by the navigator.
- **c** How does the navigator use the stars?

2 Design your own out-rigger. What are the most important features to remember?

The effect of Europeans in Micronesia

When Europeans arrived in the Pacific they had compasses and other mechanical devices for navigation. They had charts and maps too; in fact all their guides were written down.

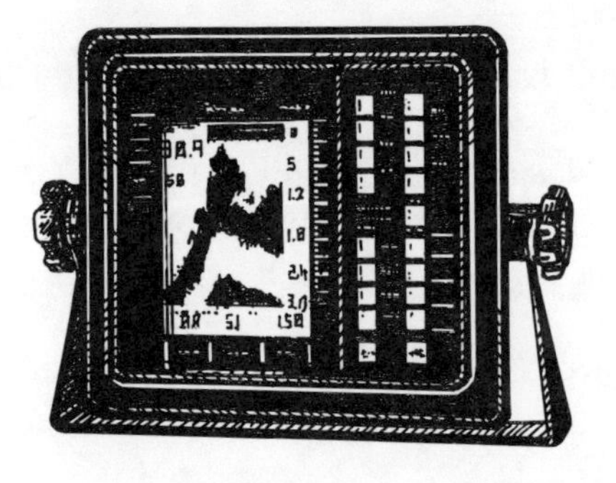

Fig. 72 Modern aids to navigation.

ACTIVITIES

Discuss in what ways the oral tradition helps to maintain the long-term survival of a culture. Do you think one's relationship or attitude to the land, sea and environment is different in an oral rather than a written tradition? Explain.

The following statements have been adapted from *Pacific Identity* (see 'Resources' below). Use them as the basis for a class discussion.

a In an oral culture, talking and learning takes place in an atmosphere of celebration or play. Only with the invention of writing and the isolation of the individual from the tribe does verbal learning and understanding itself become 'work' as distinct from play, and the pleasure or enjoyment of learning is downgraded.

b In a written tradition people learn more with the eye than with the ear. They depend on notes and books. In an oral culture, the ear has to depend on memory. As taking of notes increases under modern education systems, so the development of memory decreases and we become more dependent on computers and machines.

c Writing is absolutely essential for economics, law and government and technological development.

RESEARCH PROJECT

What sort of effect do you think the introduction of telephones, radios, television and fast radar-controlled boats and jets might have on the navigator's traditional role in the following areas?

- ▲ power and status in the village
- ▲ type of boats used
- ▲ communication
- ▲ their oral tradition
- ▲ warfare
- ▲ control of trade
- ▲ sacred places

When you have finished your response, research a Pacific culture where the role of the navigator has been affected by the introduction of modern technology.

Resources

Farrall, L. *Unwritten Knowledge*, Deakin University Press, 1984.
Frazer, H. *New Caledonia*, Peace Research Centre, Research School of Pacific Studies, A.N.U., Canberra, 1988.
Gladwin, T. *East is a Bird*, Harvard University Press, 1970.
South Pacific Social Sciences Association, *Pacific Identity,* a special issue of *Pacific Perspective* (vol. 12, no. 2) Box 5083, Raiwaqa, Fiji, 1984.
Yates, F. A. *The Art of Memory*, University of Chicago Press, Illinois, 1966.

Index

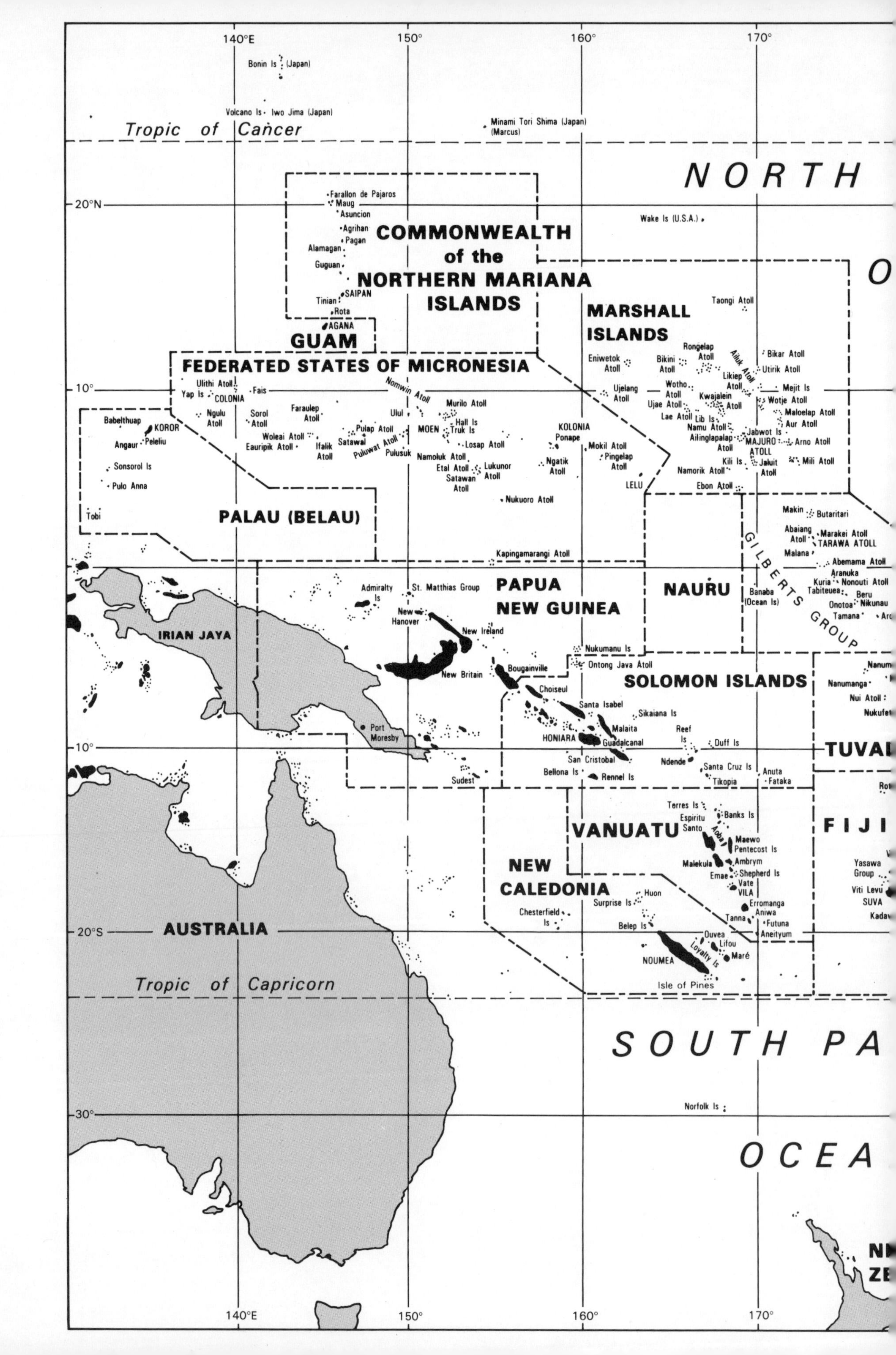
140°E
150°
160°
170°
Bonin Is (Japan)
Volcano Is
Iwo Jima (Japan)
Minami Tori Shima (Japan)
(Marcus)
Tropic of Cancer
NORTH
20°N
Farallon de Pajaros
Maug
Asuncion
Agrihan
Pagan
Alamagan
Guguan
Saipan
Tinian
Rota
AGANA
COMMONWEALTH of the NORTHERN MARIANA ISLANDS
GUAM
Wake Is (U.S.A.)
O
MARSHALL ISLANDS
Taongi Atoll
FEDERATED STATES OF MICRONESIA
Eniwetok Atoll
Bikini Atoll
Rongelap Atoll
Ailuk Atoll
Bikar Atoll
Utirik Atoll
Likiep Atoll
Mejit Is
Wotje Atoll
10°
Ulithi Atoll
Yap Is
COLONIA
Fais
Nomwin Atoll
Ujelang Atoll
Wotho Atoll
Ujae Atoll
Kwajalein Atoll
Lae Atoll
Lib Is
Namu Atoll
Maloelap Atoll
Aur Atoll
Ngulu Atoll
Sorol Atoll
Faraulep Atoll
Ulul
Murilo Atoll
Babelthuap
KOROR
Angaur
Peleliu
Woleai Atoll
Eauripik Atoll
Ifalik Atoll
Satawal
Pulap Atoll
Puluwat Atoll
Pulusuk
MOEN
Hall Is
Truk Is
Losap Atoll
KOLONIA
Ponape
Mokil Atoll
Pingelap Atoll
Ailinglapalap Atoll
Jabwot Is
MAJURO ATOLL
Arno Atoll
Kili Is
Jaluit Atoll
Mili Atoll
Namorik Atoll
Sonsorol Is
Pulo Anna
Namoluk Atoll
Etal Atoll
Satawan Atoll
Lukunor Atoll
Ngatik Atoll
LELU
Ebon Atoll
Nukuoro Atoll
Tobi
PALAU (BELAU)
Makin
Butaritari
Abaiang Atoll
Marakei Atoll
TARAWA ATOLL
Malana
GILBERTS GROUP
Kapingamarangi Atoll
Abemama Atoll
Aranuka
Kuria
Nonouti Atoll
Tabiteuea
Beru
Nikunau
Onotoa
Tamana
Aro
Admiralty Is
St. Matthias Group
PAPUA NEW GUINEA
NAURU
Banaba (Ocean Is)
New Hanover
New Ireland
IRIAN JAYA
Nukumanu Is
Ontong Java Atoll
Nanum
Nanumanga
Nui Atoll
Nukufet
New Britain
Bougainville
SOLOMON ISLANDS
Choiseul
Santa Isabel
Sikaiana Is
Port Moresby
Malaita
HONIARA
Guadalcanal
Reef Is
Duff Is
10°
TUVAL
San Cristobal
Ndende
Santa Cruz Is
Anuta
Fataka
Bellona Is
Rennel Is
Tikopia
Sudest
Rot
Torres Is
Banks Is
Espiritu Santo
Aoba I
VANUATU
FIJI
Maewo
Pentecost Is
Ambrym
Malekula
Emae
Shepherd Is
Vate
VILA
NEW CALEDONIA
Yasawa Group
Viti Levu
SUVA
Kadav
Huon
Surprise Is
Erromanga
Aniwa
Chesterfield Is
Tanna
Futuna
Aneityum
Belep Is
20°S
AUSTRALIA
Ouvea
Lifou
Loyalty Is
Maré
NOUMEA
Isle of Pines
Tropic of Capricorn
SOUTH PA
30°
Norfolk Is
OCEA
N
ZE